THE FAITH
OF THE ROMAN CHURCH

by

C. C. MARTINDALE, S.J.

GREENWOOD PRESS, PUBLISHERS
NEW YORK

PREFACE

THIS book was originally published in 1927 by Messrs. Methuen who have kindly allowed it to re-appear today, almost unaltered. It formed one volume in a series called "The Faiths", and for the sake of uniformity was called *The Faith of the Roman Church*. The title is here retained in the sense in which it is used in a popular "devotion", which speaks of ancient Saints who "delivered to us inviolate the Faith of the holy Roman Church". In this way, there is less likelihood of anyone's taking it for a wholly new book.

The General Editor of the original series, the late Dr. L. P. Jacks, asked that the books might be written in a "personal" way and not be mere theological diagrams. But while we trust we have not disguised, here and there, our personal sentiments, we hope that we have made it clear that it is not these which are the basis of belief. His sentiments may account for a man's fervour in practising his Faith; they may assist him to hold it with a new conviction: but they are not at all his reasons for believing that the Church's dogmas are true, or her commands right. A Catholic considers that he has cogent reasons for holding that the Roman Church is guaranteed by God to teach him only what is true, and to command him only what is right. He has then but to discover what she teaches and commands, and will proceed to believe the dogma, and obey the command, not only when he has no feelings about the matter, but when his feelings may be in a perfect tumult of opposition. A Catholic does not believe in the Real Presence, for example, because he feels a spiritual sweetness at the hour of Communion, nor even because he finds that Communion "helps" him (for he may not do so), but because his Teacher tells him that Christ is truly present in the Eucharist, and Authority bids him periodically approach the altar. He does not believe a dogma because he sees very clearly what it means, nor because he thinks it would be useful were it true. He may not be able to see much "use" in the doctrine of our Lord's "descent to hell", nor even accurately what it implies; he may remain for ever puzzled, intellectually, by the dogma of Creation, and the co-existence of the limited Universe with the Infinite, Necessary and Immutable. Pain may be for him to the end an ethical problem never explained. Yet he will believe duly and seek to act rightly in view of all this. He will, in short, think his personal feelings quite unimportant, since he may have good ones, or wrong ones, or none. He will beg a listener to base nothing on such things, since, he holds, they may indeed be an echo, a luminous reflection, of an objective truth, but they originate nothing, and account for nothing, save as we said for his relative ease in practising this or that duty, or enjoyment of this or that doctrine.

Yet when he approaches something of which the contents are very rich, he will not be able to attend to all of it equally, or at once; in fact, the more limited he is, the less adequate—the more lopsided, even—his appreciation of it will be. Even the hereditary Catholic may wake up, after a while, to astonishing implications in the Creed he always held. But a man who enters the Catholic world from outside—for indeed the *Res Catholica* is a World and nothing less, containing every other kind of world and a great deal more—is bound to come to it already partly formed, with his preferences, his shrinkings, his perspectives. It makes no difference whether what he brings, or what he finds, helps him or hinders him: he cannot but attend to the attractions and repulsions he experiences, or at any rate they and their consequences will continue to attend on him. Therefore any Catholic, even, will have his individual way, up to a point, of assimilating the Universal Thing.

Fully recognizing, then, the part which each man's habit of mind, or temperament, will play in his way of laying hold of any proposition, we hope first of all to indicate the intellectual substratum of the Faith—not that each Catholic explicitly concentrates on it, but he knows that something of the sort is there, and could be explained to him had he time, brains, and need for it. Without it, Catholic doctrine hangs in the air, unbased as unsupported: hence if, in this first section, we allude to Catholic doctrine, it will be as illustration, and not as sanction. Then we shall try to state what Catholic doctrine is, and then look briefly at that doctrine as it has pervaded and formed history, and as it energizes in our present world.

C. C. M.

CONTENTS

ix

PART I

FOUNDATIONS

1. MAN

RELIGION is meant for Man. Man is a restless, straining, maybe developing creature; complex and not
well harmonized within himself; inadequately adjusted
to any known environment. A Faith, then, calling itself
"Catholic", must cater for every part of man, and for
no one part at the ultimate expense of the others, or of
any other. And it must treat man "socially" as well as
individually, and in view of what he is becoming. No
one is likely to esteem him the "finished article".

Man is in part material. Catholics as such offer no
opinion as to the ultimate constitution of "matter":
enough to acknowledge that there is in us a "material
co-efficient". Useless to argue with one who maintains
we are in no sense "body". In fact, we are a sort of
animal. An animal is a thing of instincts. But instinct
cannot control itself. Yet we have that in us which
can control instinct; and in fact it is along the line of an
ever more adequate control of instinct that Man develops
and advances. Thus we have in us at least the instincts
of self-preservation, self-extension, and self-reproduction.
Whether these can be reduced to one does not matter.
Each, uncontrolled, can wreck a life. But the only
method of controlling (as opposed to coercing) them,
is to use Principles—ideas that have become ideals, and
thus, motives. Suppress an instinct out of existence
you cannot: for it is part of "you". But control it
you can, and in no other way. Thus, Brown is thirsty,

I

and likes whisky. He enters Smith's room and sees a bottle of it handy. He will certainly drink it, unless a thought controls him, such as, "This is Smith's whisky, and he might object". But he may care less about Smith's objection than about the whisky. He will then drink, unless, for example, he reflects that Smith may come in, bringing with him Jones, from whom Brown expects a job, and who, being a rabid teetotaller, is unlikely to offer the job to one whom he finds drinking in solitude. . . . So he refrains, being no less thirsty, and having the whisky no less accessible. All that has altered is his mind, and by means of it, he controls his instinct here and now. If he can't, you say he is "weak-minded". Therefore, to control instinct, to act human-wise, you need ideas that you think true, and motives that you judge important. Experience, then, shows that you have two principles in you; one, that starts in and from the body, instinct; and one that we call mind, which can have knowledge of facts other than interior ones, that can perceive relations between such facts and self, and that can present motives to a power of self-inhibition, of choosing, to a "free-able will".

Brief reflection shows us that these two principles are of essentially different orders. The printer's ink that is "music" on paper is a different *sort* of thing from the music the musician knows: the senses that pick up the material and minister it to the mind are different in themselves from thought. Plato yearned for a time when he might dispense with the twanging strings and glittering skies, and think of relations as such, and motion as such. But he could not achieve this, for these two principles are not "in us" as jewels, say, might be in a casket; they are not artificially combined. We are not body *plus* soul, but body-soul, each of us a "person", an "I". Hence even the sensualist has some sort of an idea floating about his pleasures, else he would not so much as know he was enjoying them; and the philosopher or mathematician has always to help himself out by a little imagination, annoying though it be, in order to fix his thought; and, the imagination cannot but be set going by the purest thought. We are, therefore, complex unities, "complete substances", body-souls.

Reflection upon this principle which is self-conscious and to which we owe our abstract ideas, shows that what is thus immaterial (and indeed it is at all points different and deals with a different order or reality from what is bulky and ponderable and extended and divisible and deals with similar objects), is "simple", that is, is non-extended, has no parts in a material sense, and so, cannot be destroyed. For an object to be destroyed must be exploded from within, or crushed from without —reduced, in either case, to its parts. But the immaterial has no such parts. Nor can this element in us be a "part" of some larger thing of the same nature (as a chip from a block of wood can be detached and become independent), for the same reason. We may use plenty of metaphors: this immaterial fact that is in us—call it spirit, to save time—may be named an emanation from, spark of, some greater spirit. But the metaphors suggest more that is false than what they state of true. And let us say, for the moment, that though the words "spirit", "soul", "mind" really all mean exactly the same *thing*, we use them here as follows—we say "spirit" when we mean the essential nature of that within us which we wish to distinguish from matter: we say "soul", when we allude to it as composing one whole along with matter, which here is best called "body"; and we say "mind" when we allude to the same principle, precisely, as *thinking*—that is, as functioning intelligently along with the brain. It is clear then that when the matter that composes "body" is seriously disturbed, the "mind" may, or must, cease to function; when "body" disintegrates, the soul, quite strictly as "soul", may be said to cease to be: but that "spirit", which it is, not only does not but cannot cease to be, for it is indestructible; nor can it merely merge with some vaster spirit, for it has no parts itself, nor can it become a part of what, like itself, is essentially partless.[1]

The Church's doctrine rhymes throughout with this. She has consistently taught that man is a unity, composed of body and soul, matter and spirit, and that the latter is indestructible. She has not precisely defined that the mind can know truth, fact, outside itself; but in 1347 the proposition that the mind can have certain knowledge only about itself, was condemned; that it *can*, by a process of reasoning, have certain knowledge of God has been, we shall see, defined; and that the mind can know with certainty objective fact other than itself is presupposed in all her doctrine, and the various attempts to reconcile Kantianism with theology have failed. Finally, the whole of her asceticism implies that it is man's business to gain control of himself by means of his intelligence, ever more exactly and richly conformed with truth, and developed by obedience to it. That the will is essentially free, has often been defined, especially in the time of St. Augustine, and of Jansenism.

The more generally true a man's ideas, and the more weighty his motives, the better his chance of complete and enduring self-control. I once attended a meeting "for the Reclamation of Criminals". The speeches were off the point. They dealt with: "How to make it

[1] Several critics have urged that Catholic authorities (e.g. St. Augustine) have often said that the soul "tends to nothingness" and therefore *can* be destroyed. Of course, it, like everything He created, cannot subsist without God's sustaining will: but, of its own nature, it cannot fall to pieces as the body does, for it has no pieces to fall into.

safe for other people to live near a criminal let out of
prison." The only "reclamation" of such a man must
be the alteration of his mind. But this must be positive.
A young burglar had been brought to a prelate. "Give
it up, my lad; cut it out, eliminate it," said the kindly
bishop to him. The lad tried, and passed an unbur-
glarious six months. But then, since he found no tem-
peramental outlet in drink, gambling, games or women,
he was so bored that he sought, perforce, his thrill where
he knew he would find it, and broke into five houses
that night for the joy of the thing. I said: "Your prelate
was kind: but how silly. He was emptying the boy's
head of the one thing that interested him: his one
directive idea. He should have substituted what was
more interesting than burgling." "What then? Must he
fall in love, marry, and earn dollars for his wife?" Better
than nothing. An idea, there; and a motive. But both,
how inadequate! A half-way idea: a half-time motive.
They last, while his wife lasts: suppose she dies? and
what is there, in that offered motive, to persuade him
to make his dollars honestly, if he can make them, swiftly
and safely, dishonestly? For complete success, you need
an idea that is universally true, a motive that is absolutely cogent. Do any such exist? Reason says Yes,
and the Church supports her.

2. GOD

Anthropology can find no race that does not believe
in God. Races that seemed "godless" are found to
have been concealing their beliefs from the inquisitive
explorer—what is "sacred" for them is "secret"; or,
to have been misunderstood by travellers ill-instructed
in a language itself perhaps ill-formed for such explana-
tions, or arriving primed with ideas as to what they

would or would not find. Or, the tribe had degenerated, yet revealed at last relics of religion beneath its actual superstition or ritual.

Theories, formed to explain the origin of this belief, have had no lasting success. Animism, if indeed it be the key to open every lock, should everywhere have followed the same line of development. If waving wood, blustering wind, tossing seas, or lightning, gave rise to belief in "spirits", and these became gods, and hence arose the notion of one God, this should have happened in very animistic Mesopotamia. But it did not. Assyrian animism became just polydæmonism. If ancestor-worship is the origin of god-worship, it should be noticeably so in China. But the Chinese gods are not the product of ancestor-cults, nor do ancestors there turn into the gods that should breed one God. Sir J. G. Frazer's theory, that magic everywhere underlay and turned into religion, demands that you should find at least one instance of a primitive folk, not only having magic, and no religion, but hatching a religion out of that magic. But you do not. Everywhere magic and religion co-exist and are intertwined. It is wantonly to beg the question to assert that the magical elements are the earlier, and the source of the rest. Indeed, the more a tribe degenerates, the more it collapses out of religion into magic. The whole of the *Golden Bough* is one long begging of this question. Totemism has long ago been declared a "hobby-horse and an over-ridden hobby too".

On our side, we hold it to be easy, and natural, for the intelligence to rise, from the spectacle (or direct consciousness) of the limited and dependent, to the certainty that an Independent exists, which is responsible for all the rest. To such an existence we give the name of God.

We do not propose, in what is essentially not an
apologetic book, to work out fully the lines of argument by which this may be supported. We hold them
to be perfectly valid, unless the intelligence be incapable
of knowing "fact" at all. But if it be incapable (though
even to deny that it can know truth, implies that it can
and does), it is idle to talk about religion or anything
else. We hold then that our perception of the dependent,
as all that we perceive around us, and indeed in us, is,
involves the recognition of an Independent. Idle to say
that all these dependent facts are interdependent, and
give one another support. To start with, they don't.
King Charles's execution does not depend on me. And,
they can all be "thought together" as The Dependent:
but what depends, depends on something: but this
cannot itself be dependent, else it would fall back into
the general stock of "dependent", and we must begin
again. Similarly, we observe the changeable: and this
too, in the long run, depends on the Unchanging to
account for it. To me, this conception of the moving,
the never-the-same, requiring for its foundation the
Immutable, is very attractive. And the argument that
subordinate truths or forms of reality must depend
upon higher truths not less but more real, and these,
finally, on the only Really Real, is overwhelmingly
cogent, and what Plato meant to say and perhaps did.
And there are other reasons of different orders for
holding that Humanity, in acknowledging the Existence
of God, is no mental *malade imaginaire*.

By "God" then we mean That which is self-subsistent,
by essence absolutely independent, and on which all
else totally depends. And the Vatican Council defines
this natural conclusion as true: it anathematizes one
who should deny that God "can be known with certainty by the light of human reason by means of things

created". Note how accurate is this formula. The Church does not define that this or that argument is valid, let alone the best, for knowing with certainty that God exists; it says: "by means of created things"; and, "by the natural light of human reason". It does not say that this is the only, or quickest, or easiest, or best, or final way of knowing God; nor that all men, or most, know Him by this way, or at all. But a Catholic would become a heretic were he to deny that human reason, without revelation, apart from authority, can attain certainty as to this—God exists.

This austere doctrine is of value even to Catholic experience, if only because it emancipates us from having to rely on *mere* experience. Of religious woes, sentimentalism, impressionism, is among the worst. We must not think we believe in God according as we feel, or do not feel, that He exists. Men appeal to exalted states in which they feel that "God is close to them", or "in" them.. Such states may carry great conviction even when but remembered. Still, they fade: often, memory cannot retain enough of them to make it certain that such experiences were so extraordinary after all. A man recalls he was very enthusiastic—he doesn't quite know why. And, many men have no such experiences. They cannot tell what you are talking about. Others feel thrilled at sight of dawn or stars, or sound of thunder or of waterfall; the difference is not obvious; these impressions, too, fade, cannot be recaptured, can be explained in a dozen ways that introduce no mention of a God. A Catholic holds grimly (along with authoritative teaching) to his reason, to what he has attained, especially when his emotions do not correspond. Catholics know, even, how dangerous is the cloud of emotion that may arise in them in spite of, or even because of, their thought. They resist the bias of desire, or disgust, more than ever when the object of their thought is so supra-sensible as to be essentially unimaginable, as God is.

Add this, too. The Catholic knows that he truly can think *God*, but never forgets that *he* is *thinking* God. To use, for once, a technical phrase: we have true, but analogical knowledge of God, even of the fact that He "exists". We can have "univocal" knowledge of what is, like ourselves, dependent, contingent, limited. A man may know his fellow "even as he himself is known". But God is Necessary Being. In the mere fact and way of Being He differs essentially from us: therefore nothing can be said of ourselves (or of any finite thing) and of God, in wholly the same sense. Even more strikingly true is this of the "attributes of God": for they require more human foundation for the ideas that represent them, than Being does. Emphatically, then, we can have true knowledge of God: but it remains human knowledge: a true idea of God *is* true; but the way in which what it represents is "in" God, is a way proper to God and to God alone; and that very word "in" has to be used analogically, and almost metaphorically, for God, we shall see, is a Simple Perfection; there are in Him no parts, even thinkable; and while then without any scepticism we gratefully acknowledge what we know of God, and that we know God, we humbly adore That which is beyond all our knowledge, and beyond every knowledge other than God's own knowledge of Himself.

3. GOD: HIS "ATTRIBUTES"

Human reason is, we said, apt for knowing truth. But no less apt to fly off, from any known truth, at a thousand tangents; to involve itself in a thousand false deductions. Even an untutored intelligence can and does rise, in a flash, from the spectacle of phenomena to the recognition of an Ultimate. The process of reasoning is valid, even when unconscious. But a man from the woods could, on a first astounding sight of the sea, abruptly imagine that there must be some other Ultimate to account for it: earthquake or conflagration can suggest that the great Ultimate is cruel. Hence polytheisms and mythologies. We can watch their elaboration. Few *a priori* theories are so perverse as that of the regular purification of religions towards monotheism. Religions complicate themselves, and degenerate, save among the few, where they thin out into some pale philosophy, and excepting, always, the Hebrews. Only at the end of Egyptian history have ibis and crocodile to be worshipped, and the fields become haunted by the ghosts of a myriad mummied cats.

God, we have said, is the absolutely Independent. Now that which is dependent, is limited; for it is limited by that on which it depends. Similarly, the limited is ever the dependent. Therefore, the Absolute must needs be the Un-Limited, and by brief reasoning is seen thus to be Infinite. Therefore God is One, and can be no other; for, there cannot be two Infinities; each would lack the other's selfhood, and so, neither would be infinite. But the Infinite is also the Eternal, else it would exist "in time", and be limited: and, the Omnipresent, else again, it would be limited. Moreover, it must be at least what we mean by Spiritual: for, there is always a series in matter—this after that; this outside of that. Finally· where there is imperfection, there is no infinity. Therefore God is the All-Perfect.

Now that which is the total cause of anything—and the Absolutely Independent has all things else dependent upon it for their very existence—contains the qualities

of that thing, either as such, as paint in brush, or, in a
better way, as portrait in the mind of the artist. It is
not there in terms of paint, but better. But among the
qualities of which we are aware in ourselves, we reckon
intelligence and will. Therefore these are, too, in God,
though in a better way, namely, as in their source, in-
dependently, and infinitely. Therefore God is said to
"know", because we know; yet not as we know—
fragmentarily, successively, but, in one infinite knowledge
which is Himself. And, God "can"; is Will, since we
can will; yet again, not as we will, by tedious effort,
and dependently on motive. Finally, enough to say,
God is Good, and is Personal. Good, because Evil is
not a perfection, nor subsistent, but the privation of a
perfection that should be present. But, in the Infinite,
there can be no gap, no inadequacy. And Personal,
because there is in Him, as we saw, every perfection;
but we experience certain perfections that enable us to
speak of ourselves as persons; we do not so call a table,
nor even a dog. Therefore God is perfect with all those
perfections too; again, not as they are in us, limitedly,
but infinitely, and as in their source. This then, and more,
had we space to dwell on it, the Church defines, though
to know it we need not appeal to her definition. "God",
says the Vatican Council, in the wake of many another,
is "One, Eternal, Immense, Incomprehensible, Infinite in
intelligence and will and every perfection, . . . and, above
all things that exist or can be conceived other than Himself, ineffably exalted."

Let none say that this is a God made in man's image,
nor mention "anthropomorphism". Rather we have
seen that man is, in his way, "theomorphic". We should
be guilty were we to say that God is wise, good, *exists*
as man is wise, or good, or exists. But that is just what
we do not do. We say but that what is in man, so far

as it is a perfection, must be in God, but in God's way which is not ours. Even when we say a man is a "person", to some extent we think of him as an "individual", with a good dose of the negative about him—he is *not* any of the other individuals that populate the world. When we say "Person" of God, we mean none of these negations. Bound to speak analogically, we say that the perfections ascribed to God, are truly ascribed to Him, yet, since our concept of them is derived from humanity, inadequately asserted of Him. God *is* what a human person is, but "is" it better. Our idea of God then is not just negative: we but negate negations.

We may add, without arguing our points, that many notions about God are forbidden to the Catholic. Indeed, they should be to any thinking man. The limited, fairly benevolent, very impotent, none too wise a god re-invented by a popular novelist, was an unthought-out notion. Mr. Wells played with it and left it as a cat leaves a half-dead mouse in the back garden of a suburban villa. It means nothing to a Catholic. Again, the expanding and shrinking god, hastily borrowed by Theosophists from misunderstood Indian lore—the god who (from one point of view) develops into the innumerable forms of the universe, or (from another) degenerates into them and then re-absorbs himself into his inexpressible self-hood—is likewise unintelligible. For the Infinite is the Immutable. Nor can we "think" a god who *manifests himself* in myriad ways, so that the only reality is God, and all else illusion. After all, there must be someone or something to suffer the illusion, but the Infinite Spirit that God is, cannot be deluded, nor split into parts, so that in part of himself he suffers any such thing. No kind of Pantheism is permitted to the Catholic, even when he may use a language that sounds pantheist, as when a mystic exclaims that God is all. At the back of such outcries is the Catholic dogma that God is not the universe, nor the universe God.

Since this is not a book of controversy nor even apologetics, we have said so much only to show that the Catholic Faith includes a core of reason, and is emphatically not an affair of sentiment, still less of taking leaps in the dark, or of starting with God "because one must start somewhere". Still less must we answer difficulties. That the idea of Creation is "difficult", who shall doubt? But once you have said that God is freely the author of the Universe, you have stated the positive content of the dogma of Creation. Once the covering idea is clear, that God is an Infinite Spirit, Immutable, Necessary, and sovranly Free, it becomes clear, too, that the world of limited, contingent, and often mechanical objects, cannot have "emanated" from Him, nor be part of Him, nor He. Pain, too, is a problem. Who ignores the popular dilemma—God must be impotent, or evil; for either He cannot help pain, or He will not? Well, if we have the irreducibly true covering certainty that God, being Infinite, *must* be both all-powerful, and all-good, every isolated fact that seems to contradict that either does not contradict it, or, is not a fact. There is no need for us to understand, nor possibility of our understanding, the exact relation of every detail to the whole. Who should understand the meaning of each thread, each knot, at the back of a piece of a still-unfinished tapestry? Once we know that a Master-Weaver unerringly is weaving, it is alone reasonable and just that we assign what we cannot understand, not to His incompetence, but to ours.

Even so, some will sincerely say that they prefer their untutored apprehensions of God—what they "feel" He must be—to these abstract considerations. Well, that the latter are not enough, is for a Christian doubly certain:

first, because they are hard to come by; and, because Christ revealed a very different order of truths about God. But even as such, are these considerations religiously neutral? We remember reading them, magnificently (we were thinking) set forth in William James's *Varieties of Religious Experience*. We turned the page, and found, aghast, that he could see "nothing in" them—could anyone, he asked, be stirred by that sort of abstraction? Deprecate the hunt for emotions as we would, yet "Alas", we in our turn asked, "Could any man remain, then, so utterly on the surface as this American philosopher seemed to do? So fail to realise the profundity of what seemed to him mere diagram?" Could there really be a soul which, in hours when life so flickers by that the poor mind can scarcely assimilate one item in it before the thing is lost and we have to sigh—"Had I but guessed: had I but understood and used what was to my hand"—a soul, then, that never leans back with gratitude upon the thought of God's Immutability? when the best that we have endures but long enough to die, that cannot plunge itself into the thought of God's Eternity? when things fall into fragments in our very hands, that cannot rest on His Infinity? in hours of desperate separation, that cannot pacify itself in the certainty of His Omnipresence? A presence, too, that is totally within myself, since God is not *spatial*, but is all of Him everywhere, just as His Eternity is not indefinite duration, but all of it Now? For what is not the consequence of that Totality of God in me? When I know myself helpless in face of work to be done, spiritual work especially, to know too that I have, if I will but use it, Omnipotence within me: when life bears in upon me the precarious, most partial truth of my wisest judgments, my keenest intuitions, and when the abysses of my ignorance gape suddenly at my feet, and I realize, above all,

the unbridged chasm between my self and the self of
my dearest friend, to recall God's Omniscience, to know
that *He* knows, and that about this I cannot err. Above
all, when I see with horror the spottedness of my purest
thought, the specks of rottenness in what I dreamed was
undefiled within me, the decaying fibres in the very
marrow of my will—*then* to recall the Infinite Goodness
of God, the clarity of His Holiness. To me it is not
strange that during the night of his unassisted, unbelieved-
in dying, St. Ignatius was heard repeating, again and
again, the lonely Name of GOD. He who knew of, and
could make his whole self over to, Life itself, the True
and Living God, could find no meaning in the act of
dying save that it was a passage to the complete and
adequate Joy, that he knew already, but obscurely still,
in the twilight of reason and of faith.

We have spent long on this section of our book, because
all else in the Catholic Creed is folly, if it be not known
as based upon this knowledge, won from reason and
re-taught by Faith, that there exists, truly, GOD—One,
Eternal, Infinite, Changeless, Omnipresent, All-Powerful,
All-Wise, All-Good; Personal; our Creator, and hence
our Lord and our Last End.

4. GOD: HIS LAW

The word "Lord" lifts us into the next section of
our statement. A man, sufficiently knowing himself,
sufficiently knowing God, sees at once that he is responsible to God. For God creates with a purpose.
Only a fool acts at random or haphazard. The All-
Wisdom is not a fool. Nor is it possible for God to
act clumsily, in the rough, without troubling about
details. For each soul God has a purpose. But that
purpose—what each man is "meant to be"—must be

good, for in the All-Good is no evil. And that purpose must be appropriate to the nature of man, must be achievable by intelligent choice, else "man" has not achieved it, but will have been coerced, that is, have acted inhumanly.

For man, then, to neglect this achievement, is folly, for he neglects what alone can be his supreme good: criminal folly, if deliberate, and only short of defiance. Defiance it is, when a man realizes that the purpose carries with it a vocation: God cannot remain neutral to the achievement of His own purpose. Man then knows that he "ought" to fulfil himself: he experiences that sense of obligation which cannot be confused with anything else. "I ought" is essentially different from "I would like", "It would pay", "I cannot help it". This is not due to environment: a man often has to defy that; to tear himself right out of it. Nor is "conscience", by which we mean the practical judgment of what I ought here and now to do, and *not* a mere all-over-ish feeling—my own law against my self. For what I enact, I can rescind. Of all substitutes for true Obligation, the shoddiest seems to us Ancestral Instinct, accumulated hereditary bias, or what not, since continually a man has to run counter to it; to-day, he almost makes his pride out of doing so. A Catholic then holds that life is throughout responsible, explicitly so, once a man has reflected on his nature and its origin. A man then has for first duty the *not* running counter to such knowledge as he has, and then, the discovery of as much more truth as he can get, so as to advance more quickly and firmly to what he should become.

The soul—the self—then grows by thinking and choosing right: for thoughts and choices are not things you have, but things you are. A man is intrinsically altered by his deliberate acts, especially the interior ones. Even sins are more what you make yourself, than what you do. An outside act may prolong, intensify, or "fix" the interior mind or will: but it is interiorly that the spiritual act is consummated. Can a man go so far as to exhale, as it were, his whole personality into a choice that he knows to be wrong? Make his self wholly wrong? We cannot deny it. Similarly, he would be able to express his total self in an act wholly good. Perhaps psychology cannot quite answer that. But just as research always shows men to us as experiencing this sense of obligation towards their "Ultimate", so men have always tended to allow that they might reach an "extreme" in either direction—make themselves "all-through" bad, or good. We cannot deny the possibility of "enduring consequences". Men like to forget so soon as they may what has made them feel ashamed, or lowered. Forget it they may, but the consequences abide, till rectified. Others will say: "I will begin again." Impossible. One can but continue thence, whence one left off, if ever one does leave off, since every moment spent in a state worse than its preceding one, worsens the man yet more. The "lie in the soul" splits deeper apart ideas once easily associated; the sick love and choice enfeebles the very power to grip that good thing still ready to the hand. Then the good object of choice retires and may become invisible, or at least intangible. Let none talk of conscience as of a stable factor to be relied upon for telling the truest and the best. It can hesitate; be stifled, "talked down"; be distorted, falsified almost wholly. We have watched it. It is a ghastly spectacle. Either, as St. Paul diagnosed in the pagan world, the continuous misuse of that light which all possess may bring men into a state that is sub-natural— where the soul's whole ideal is manifestly wrong—or, too intelligent to succumb to such negation, men remain seeing what is good, but lacking power or even wish to pursue it. They stare, sick at heart, at the old vision that has ceased to summon them. "*Virtutem videant, intabescantque relicta.*"

Parenthetically, we suggest that all well-founded modern psychology regarding the mind, its disintegrations, constructions, complications, sublimations, can well be correlated with what we have said. What the psychologist registers as a psychic wound, or disease, *is* so: once the idea of God is seen as philosophically valid, the disease indeed remains, but can be viewed as sin, the moment it is willed. No idea is comparable with that of God for enabling the mind to reconstruct itself, and would that we heard so much of psycho-synthesis as we do of psycho-analysis. But all depends on the sick man holding the idea as *true*: once he thinks it but a useful fiction, it ceases to operate. You cannot bluff yourself indefinitely. No suicide is so complete as that of the psychiatrist who lets it be known that he considers general ideas to be merely who knows what Brocken-spectres thrown off by who knows what self on to who knows what clouds. He provides swift ruin for his method—for who will continue to use ideas that he is taught are illusory?—and he does grave damage to society. It is manifest that a frightful shock has been administered to the none too steady equilibrium of our race, by the vulgarization of the idea that the only reality is instinct, and that the ideas which serve to make instinct harmless, or even socially useful, are ghosts.

Already, then, in the philosophy underlying Catholic dogma, we see that "wrong-doing" is possible, and has the quality of "sin", of offence against God who has set one perfect destiny before each. "Sin" is disobedience to no tyrannical, arbitrary command. God simply cannot admit that there is no difference between actions, even in the long run: that it all comes to the same in the end. . . . What we do, we become; and according to what we are, is our influence, and the most private act of good or ill affects all with whom we come in contact, if only because sin incapacitates us from doing the good we should. But it does more. All life is inter-communicative. A sin vibrates to the extreme of the spiritual universe: and, if there be no end to that, sin, unless rectified, itself has no end. The consequences abide, in the sinner, who has spoiled himself, and in the world, that he has helped to mar and to unmake. This is no pessimism. We indicate but a possibility: the whole Christian revelation consists of what helps to avert such a disaster. But we are speaking of the background of that revelation: and we insist that what weakens the meaning of "sin" is a tragedy for each soul, and a crime against society. There is no substitute. The Catholic, then, holds that for each man, Catholic or not, there is but one quite right course in life, and that is, to seek to know God's will, and to act according to it; and, that there is but one disaster, Sin.

But this negative view of life—the *not* going counter to God's purpose—*is* but negative. We have to offer God worship, that is, the complete recognition of His Supremacy by means of all that is in us that can express it. Men have always definitely worshipped. The fact has issued into some of the noblest, and some of the most grotesque, most horrible phenomena of history. A sufficient basis for "prayer"—what Catholics call "the raising of the mind to God"—is the simple fact that two intelligences, if in contact, can interact. God is wholly present in our souls: He cannot be unconscious of us: it remains for us to put ourselves actively into "presence" with Him. Moreover, God is active and takes the initiative in all things: in a sense, we must resist, if we do not pray: we speak of God "answering" us: it is truer to say that prayer is our answer to His endless solicitation of our mind and will. But man's sense of dependence inevitably makes him wish to express this, in gesture, or outcry, or any other manifestation, since man is exterior as well as soul. And he expresses it most readily in the shape of a gift that is a giving-*back*—an acknowledgment. What he is, he symbolizes by what he has—that over which he has "extended his personality". An agricultural folk will feel this first in regard of grain or fruit; a pastoral one will look to animals. Hence in part, or chiefly, the universal practice of offering those gifts which are of the essence of "sacrifice". And even when no sense of sin is involved, when men seek but to give a "due", there is a tendency to destroy what you offer; not that God, or the god, likes the destruction as such, but that the man may feel that what is given, is given totally and irrevocably. The distinction between this sort of gift and every other is soon appreciated. Further, the real sense that what I give stands for my self, quickly explains the sacrifice not merely of my property, but of my son, in whom more than all else "I" am; hence those tragic foundations of town or house or bridge "in" a first-born son, and the little cists of babies' bones within them. Logic would demand self-oblation in the completest sense: hence not only ritual suicides, but ritual mutilations in which the "life-blood" flows, or the power of reproduction is destroyed. Into such hideous aberrations will the true and noble idea divagate, if unguided; as for mind, so for act. And by reaction, the view of that god who accepts, and therefore must be presumed to like, or exact, such offerings, itself degenerates.

The Catholic Faith therefore involves certain absolutely necessary notions, which the intelligence can co-naturally strike out for itself, but which that Religion may define, elucidate, and control. But we have first to understand what alone makes the rest intelligible—that Man is a complex unit; a body, perishable; and a spirit, intelligent and free-able; yet, one person; and, that spirit is indestructible. That God exists, and is what we have said of Him; that He created Man for a purpose, ultimately, no doubt, His own glory, but a glory to be attained rightly by way of man's relative perfection, a perfection reached by the conformity of his human intellect with divine truth, of his human will with the Will of God. Being free, man can refuse so to conform himself: he can attend to and pursue something less than that. But he ought to do otherwise, and can do otherwise, especially if by "prayer" he puts himself into contact with the very Source of wisdom, power, and goodness. And to this Source of his being he must offer a total homage: all that he has and is must be referred to its Origin; and this reference will express itself in Worship, and the supreme act of worship is sacrifice; and this worship should be collective, since man is social as well as individual.

REVELATION

1. CHRIST

IF THEN it be so important for man to know what God's purpose with regard to him is, and to take the means necessary to achieve it, success cannot be impossible. But there are two impossibilities: one absolute and theoretical; one practical or, we may call it, moral. Thus many a truth is attainable by human intellect which no one, in the circumstances, will attain, or that most men in their circumstances will never attain. If such truths be needed for the fulfilment of man's purpose, God must add sufficient help for him to reach them. For example: it is almost inevitable, as we said, for man to get some sufficient knowledge that God exists; but, we implied, almost impossible for him not to err in his subsequent deductions. Given the accumulating and confusing mistakes of human thought: the distorting effect upon human vision of centuries of sin: the reign of formula and fashion, frivolity or revolt, it has become most unlikely that the average man will arrive with any rapidity, clarity or security at the developed truth. There is then a parallel probability, indeed a moral certainty, that God will provide some outside help, both for intellect and will. We leave to one side the possible existence of truths which in their nature wholly outpass human intelligence (so far as discovering them goes) and which yet God wishes us to know. Supernatural revelation would, in their case, be absolutely necessary. But while our reason cannot prove that there are *no* such truths, yet it cannot prove that there *are*, though a decent modesty will surmise that there well may be, and that our intelligence is not fit to exhaust all truth whatsoever. But with such truths we are not here dealing.

The Catholic then admits that there may be truths that God reveals to men because man would otherwise be unlikely to get the amount of truth he needs; and will not deny that there may be truths which absolutely require revelation if they are to be known at all. Nor can we show that the intelligence is unable to receive such a revelation, for why should it be incapable of instruction? nor again, that God cannot instruct the intelligences He has created, and that, in many ways. We say then that if we seriously need light, God is morally sure to give it, and presumably, in a way that suits our human nature wholly, that is, so as to satisfy our material, moral, spiritual, and even social needs. Neither in God, then, nor in man, is there anything that precludes the possibility of revelation; and there is much in God, and in man, and in the truths valuable to man's final end, that makes such revelation probable; and, there may be truths that make it necessary.

But if a divine act, concerning us, is probable, it is our duty to seek out whether it has occurred. And since God *could* have given such help to each individual for his private use, but is more likely, as we said, to attend to the whole nature of man, we turn with a certain good will towards those many persons who, throughout history, have claimed to offer to groups of men, or to all men, a divine revelation. In a sense, all "religions" claim to have been revealed. They all contain "authority". Even in sober, workaday religions like the Persian and the older Roman, behaviour was regulated not a little by authority. Omens, sacrifices, were not just invented, but "given". Religions of enthusiasm, like parts of the Greek worship, and still more the Oriental ones, were shot through with "revelation". And great men have claimed to be the special mouthpiece of the Invisible. Must we then go hat in hand to each, asking to scrutinize his credentials? Interminable task, as even Lucian saw. For us, it is but sensible to begin with what is nearest and most challenging—with Christ rather than with Krishna or Confucius. And we save much time. If Christ makes good His claim to be God's unique Spokesman, well, He has made it good: we need go no further. If He fails so to do, and if few others have made so exclusive and exhaustive a claim as He, the field will at least be narrowed; or if no one else has, we may be inclined to think that God has chosen some other method of revelation, if any.

There are many ways of approaching Christ—none, perhaps, illicit. Best, to approach Him by many: to form a "cumulative argument", one, that is, not of simple addition, but consisting of a complexus of considerations, each of which, placed in contact with the others, forthwith modifies them and ends by forming a vital unit. Notice that no such argument is coercive, but it issues into a "moral certainty", which does not mean mere probability, but one that warrants a prudent man giving his assent with security. In no part of historical argument is the evidence "necessary" as metaphysical truth is necessary. There is the possibility of denying evidence: the will enters here: we may so dislike a conclusion that we deny or resist the premises. Hence no argument for the Claims of Christ can give us metaphysical certainty this way or that, nor are they even meant to "prove" His Divinity as such. But, then, neither do they appeal to authority other than historical evidence, any more than anything we have so far said does. They assume no inspiration of the Scriptures; they appeal to no teaching of the Church. And we recall that we are, here, but indicating a line of approach: we work nothing out; save in passing, we do not defend what we say.

Morally and historically, the phenomenon of the "Christian Folk" in mid-second century, within the Roman Empire, is such as to rivet to it our attention and to make us ask how it came there. We want to know how slaves, great ladies, lawyers, soldiers, merchants, philosophers, actors, priests, men and women belonging not only to every layer of society but to disparate nations and races—the volatile Gaul, the still-grave Roman, the degenerate conceited Greek, the still-half-savage Briton, the harsh Spaniard, the caustic Italian, the frantic Asiatic, the still-haughty Egyptian—how all these came to have a *common mind*, transcending these enormous differences, and a common conviction, so that they were ready to die for the thing they thought. Had you asked any individual among them what accounted for him, always he would have said: "Jesus of Nazareth." Only a desire to prove this phenomenon other than unique, provides you with parallels. There is only one rival worth mentioning—Islam. But note that a man had everything to lose by becoming a Christian: he was suspected of every anarchy, mental, moral and social: the Mohammedan meant to lose nothing; or, if lose he had to, he would do it only after fighting his utmost to keep it. Not such, the Christian martyrs. The Christian Folk, then, a unique phenomenon, insists that we look to its cause, that is, Christ, as to something quite outside the ordinary.

Consider next the Jews. To do so, we must regard their literature, I confess without fear, as massively reliable: not as "inspired" nor inerrant, but as truth-fully indicating a line of vital development that is unique. Certainly the nation is unique. A group, detached millenniums ago from a vast Empire established in wealth, art, territory, science, religion, antiquity, melts into the West, reappears on shores destined to be "Mediterranean", twice retires under stress of starvation into Egypt and yet is not absorbed there in the heyday of her glory, returns, and under the formative power of a mighty personality, Moses, becomes a Nation; hacks its way into a land of hostile tribes and for a space, under a shepherd boy who became an outlaw and then a king, achieves importance on a rock by which war and commerce swept or crawled between the mighty empires to north and to south. Battered thereafter into nothingness, you would suppose, by Babylonian, Persian, Græco-Syrian, Roman, its land reduced to a city and its city to a shrine, it yet is setting one of the gravest of problems to the politicians of to-day. A nation that gave to the world no art, no science, no philosophy, no system of law, nor of political nor social theory, produced nothing but a Religion expressing itself in a millennium of literature whereof tiny shreds survive. A Religion differing from all others, since it pursued a steady course of purification and spiritualization, in sheer despite of the people's temperament; that faced ever to the future, seeing it in terms of Vocation and of Promise; that narrowed ever its vision from nation, to tribe, to clan, to family, and to one Individual, while spreading out its field of contemplation till it included the whole world and saw a Kingdom of Righteousness that should be eternal and universal under that Messiah. And Himself was so human that He could be born in one named town; and so more than human that He stood in solitary extra-cosmic relation to the God of Heaven and earth. All this is unique: and if the convergent lines of assertion are not knotted together in the person of Jesus of Nazareth, Hebrew history remains but a chaos of unsolved riddles: but, if they be so recapitulated, it receives its adequate explanation, so that we hold that while history since Christ looks definitely back to Him, history before Him looks towards Him, so that He is at least cosmo-centric. Like this is no one else.

Along such lines advances the "argument from prophecy", which includes prediction but is not exhausted by it. Nor can any *a priori* objection that "prophecy cannot happen" carry the least weight with anyone who thinks of God as we do. God is outside of time, and has complete knowledge of all that is, and as it is, and can communicate this to any limited intelligence that He wills, and when and as He wills.

Christ, further, worked Miracles. By a miracle we mean in general an event that the senses can perceive and that totally exceeds the forces that construct, by their energizing, our universe. Within the earthly career of Jesus, such events should be regarded furthermore as "signs", signs that is of the truth of His Messianic claims, and indeed, as a progressive series, culminating in His physical reappearance, alive, after physical death, and also, in their total setting, which includes His own character and that of His doctrine.

That Christ claimed to work miracles is undisputed. That the evangelists thought so too, is no less certain: impossible for criticism so to extract the miraculous thread from the web of the gospels as to leave a mere naturalistic foundation behind. Nor is it disputed that the early apostolic preaching offered anything but the Resurrection as supreme proof of the seal set by God upon His Spokesman.

It used to be said that miracles did not happen, because they could not; and that they could not, since they would involve the violation of a law of nature; this perfectly silly contention involved a confusion between "law" in the sense of "dictate", and in the sense of a

generalization of the intelligence. Certain phenomena
were seen to follow one another in similar circumstances,
and a sort of personification, Nature, was put forward
who ordained, apparently, that this should be so. Men
of science felt themselves insulted by a suggestion that
the sequences observed might not always subsist. When
the sequence went wrong, "unknown causes" were
appealed to on the assumption that God anyway must
not be involved. So far has the reaction against this
Victorian complacency gone, that men of science who
philosophize seem to tend, now, to deny the existence
of any "laws" at all; every possible generalization is
but a hypothesis to be constantly attacked and corrected
by the very men who formed it. We have actually heard
it urged by distinguished men of science, that science
and religion do not and cannot clash, since each provides
you only with hypotheses, all true up to a point but no
further, all to be revised some day, and able, perhaps,
some day to be harmonized. But at least materialism is
done with: spiritual facts are recognized as facts, and
must enter into any synthesis. Meanwhile, we hold
that within definite areas, trustworthy generalizations can
be and have been formed: we can say that the elements
that compose our world will interact similarly in similar
circumstances, differently in different ones. All depends
on the nature or origin of the difference. Thus a stone
lying on the ground will continue to lie there unless
something or someone moves it. An earthquake will
set it rolling; but nothing else happens to it save what
is due to its weight and the incline. But if you find it
to have become the capital of a pillar in a cathedral,
you know that an architect and a sculptor have conspired
to get it there. No "law" has been defied; but two
disparate laws—that of the stone, and that of a mind—
have been caused to interact. Had the law of the stone—

for example, its quality of resistance—been "defied",
it might have crumbled beneath the weight now placed
upon it, or resisted the chisel. Had the architect gone
mad, the cathedral would have fallen down. So a result
has come about that never could have done so, had stone
lacked sculptor, or sculptor stone, or had either "dis-
regarded" the "law" proper to the other, let alone to
itself. Hence since God is the supreme intelligence, He
cannot possibly be accused of "disregarding" any "law
of nature" if He acts on the physical universe in a way
which is proper both to Himself and to it, unless we
startlingly declare that God, having created things as
they are, has nothing left to do, can conceive no richer,
more total harmony, can take no action towards producing
it. We deny that if He does, there is so much as even
an interruption in nature, unless the history of the stone
is to be conceived as wantonly interrupted by the architect.
True, it has been urged that such alterations in the
"normal" sequence of phenomena "must not be allowed",
else science would become impossible. Nonsense. *Even
if* all the events that have claimed to be miracles *were*
miracles, have they interfered with science? Obviously
not. At best science can but say that phenomenon *a*
will be followed by phenomenon *b* in similar circumstances, and it can always go on saying so, even if miracles
begin to happen daily; and science is not so privileged
as to exact that circumstances never must be altered, lest
his field of observation be disturbed even for one man
once in a hundred years. As well say that the universe
exists for any departmental student. It has even been
advanced that were God to work a miracle for so and
so, He would be favouritizing him—be a regular Sultan
of a God, of whom you never could tell what He might
not do next. As if the human intelligence were likely to
know all the antecedents and consequences, during all

time, including the supernatural ones, of a miracle! As if God would work a miracle or do anything else, without a far more perfect order being intended by Him thus to come about. No. The architect, by causing his intelligence duly to act upon the stone, raises it to a new order of being, to exist as part in an organic whole, an element in a thing of eternal intellectual beauty, soliciting moreover from the spectator a new responsibility of appreciation, just as a miracle must create new obligations for one who experiences it in himself or in another. The moral world is enlarged: the spiritual horizon made wider: the soul is new-vitalized in depth and in reach.

Certainly this description of miracles, when applied to the Messianic ones, seems academic and narrowed in scope, but it is no worse for that. Certainly we should like to linger over the human tenderness with which Christ healed the sick, but it was not as doctor of the body that He came. And certainly, interesting avenues open themselves before the psychological explorer, with problems far less vulgar than those alluded to, descried on each new horizon. But while far from fearing, indeed, welcoming as we do, psychology, this is not the place for it. And while we rejoice to see how the Love of God not only has created and preserves the world, but invades and floods it by means of the Incarnation and its consequences, and steals exquisitely into it through every chink and cranny that faith may open to its workings, neither must we here speak of the Love of God or of the Incarnation. We have but wished to state that to say that miracles are "impossible" seems to us absurd; to say they are "undesirable", a sort of spiritual brattishness; and that when they are offered as, say, an attestation of a doctrine claiming to be divinely revealed, they involve God's veracity. God cannot go guarantee for a lie. The event is both sign and seal, supremely so in the case of the

Resurrection. And it may be chiefly because of their whole circumstances that miracles are best recognizable, although, as we said, certain events can be judged as totally transcending the complexus of forces energizing in the physical universe.[1]

We mentioned "cumulative proof". This is here to the point. If a man, who seemed to be theme of prophecy, or worker of miracle, yet proved to be of no special personal worth, nor teacher of any new or precious doctrine, we should be so surprised as to assume we had made a mistake somewhere—either that the personal or doctrinal values were escaping us, or, that we had misjudged the evidence for what seemed like prophecy or miracle. But if we find in Christ a transcendent character and also doctrine, not only each of these pours light on to and into the other (for, we should have been discouraged as to the doctrine had the life been manifestly out of keeping with it, and we might have regarded the history as an idealization had the doctrine been stale or inept), but the Life being what it was, we are warned to see more in the prophecies than else we might have; and the doctrine being what it is, we are the readier to find it prepared and sanctioned even by miracle.

This implies that the method consisting in cutting Christ's doctrine up into a number of sentences and

[1] For the sake of completeness, we add that the Church has condemned the view that miracles cannot happen, have not happened, and can never be recognized. Yet she exacts no belief in any "ecclesiastical miracle", those, that is, other than what the Scriptures guarantee—worked, for example, during the Church's history by Saints, or at Lourdes. This in no way permits us to treat such events lightly: that would probably imply an enfeebled view of the whole question of miracle. Personally, we are prevented from an almost pessimist estimate of human faith and nearness to God, resulting in the rareness of miracle, by the reflection that miracles are indeed meant largely as "signs", as striking occurrences "adapted to the average intelligence" (Vatican Council, session III, chapter 3) and must be rare for that very reason. Else they would "shock" no one, nor lead men's minds to anything further than the miracle, as they are meant to do, and as our Lord meant His own to do.

then seeking verbal parallels to these up and down the
records of other ancient systems, is a bad and an out-
grown one. Place the New Testament documents beside
those other ones, as wholes, and living wholes, and
the perfect difference needs no arguing. Still less can we
thus unweave Christ's life into mere threads of incident,
and place these alongside "similar" incidents in the
myths of who knows what Buddha, Zarathustra, Krishna,
Mithra, and so forth. Not only the incidents, historically
assessed, have no real similarity about them, not only,
for example, is it idle to compare the story of Christ's
birth with the birth-myths of any one of these, but, just
here we have been talking rather about character, and
those who used thus to operate with incidents, appeared
unable to take character and spiritual worth into account
at all. Anyhow, this preposterous method survives only
as a relic of conceited Victorianism, nor is it much
attended to nowadays.

A student then can move, if he will, along these lines
(or others) to the point when it becomes prudent for him,
without having once appealed to authority or even sentiment, to confess that Jesus Christ was God's guaranteed
Spokesman, and that what He taught was therefore
Truth and it alone. And part of that Teaching was,
that it was unique: the "aerolite" fallen from the "skies
of John" into Matthew's territory, is as good synoptic
rock as anything else in the first three gospels—"No
man fully knoweth the Father save the Son, and he to
whom the Son shall will to reveal Him." And the Apostles,
confessing that in "no other name" should mankind
reach salvation, showed that they well grasped the
universality and exhaustiveness of Christ's claim.

A very limited assertion has, so far, been made—not,
that Christ is God, but that He is God's Man, God's
guaranteed Spokesman, though the corollary, that what

He teaches is true and authoritative, is enough to differentiate His teaching from every subjective mood that may be ours, however strongly it should sway us. Note, too, that we have said nothing positive, so far, as to the truth or value of pagan cults, but only that they are transcended in kind by Christianity. Nor have we said that all men, or most, arrive by this path, or this one alone, or most often or most easily, to faith in Christ, but that with this for substratum, faith is not unreasonable, is, indeed, so reasonable as to make disbelief less reasonable, more almost a matter of disinclination rather than of intelligent conviction. The apologetic of a faith is other than the faith itself: the ladder to a roof is other than the roof, than the view to be seen thence, than the life to be spent up there. Above all, we have not said, God help us, that it is in this way that the Catholic (or anyone else, we suppose) "knows Christ"; that knowledge, please God, is that of a man who knows his friend. But, included in the Catholic knowledge is the certainty that Christ's appeal is not merely to emotion or even intuition, but to all that is in man, and will not contradict downright intelligence, nor "evidence", but that these too must play their part in the total knowledge of Himself. In this section, then, arid as the considerations may have seemed, they have not been academic merely, nor extrinsic to the believer, nor to the writer, and in consequence, none of this could be quite omitted. And if it be thought that such "arguments" are positively grimy with age, well, aged they are, but to us they shine with the reflection of an immemorial human light, and are incandescent with the interior radiance of Truth.

2. THE CHURCH

We hold that Christ made it clear that He intended to be not only believed, but understood. Though He declared His doctrine gradually, and gently, yet ultimately He did so most uncompromisingly, and never hinted that the alternative interpretations that could be put on what He said—as they can be on nearly all things spoken— were equally admissible. There is, of course, a philosophy of "uncertainty"; but we have said that the intelligence can arrive at the truth that is suitable to it, and is meant to do so. There is, too, nowadays, the religion of uncertainty: it acts on the idea that Christ left us uncertain, meant so to leave us, and implied thereby that it was good for us to be uncertain. We fear that this has been invented by those who *are* uncertain, cannot see how to cease to be, might feel awkward if they did cease to be, and require to justify themselves in their own eyes as much as in those of others. They cannot but acknowledge that if Christ meant us to be certain, He must have provided us with a vehicle for that certainty. But this would involve grave obligations, not shirked consciously by all, or perhaps by any, but unconsciously left under the horizon. We hold that Christ offered emphatically certain doctrines about Himself, adding credentials. He refused to coerce the mind or will of His listeners, but He was quite alien from the notion that what He offered could be accepted by emotion only, or good will, or even intellectually provided you might for ever re-cast and re-state it as years went on. He taught certain things as true, meaning them to be held for ever as true, and in the sense in which He taught them. They mattered so much to Him, that He was willing to die rather than not teach them; and so much to us, that our salvation is involved in our acceptance or rejection of them. Hence He will have arranged for us to know them—for His hearers of every age and land, among whom we are.

He might have left the meaning of His doctrine to individual experience: but He did not: no document suggests that He did; moreover, when men do trust to their private inspiration, experience, or "conscience", they arrive at mutually exclusive conclusions, which can be supposed not to matter only if the true meaning of Christ's doctrine does not matter. But it makes an enormous difference if Christ rose from the dead only in the sense that His influence startlingly revived, almost as though Abraham might be said to "rise" with each recrudescence of Zionism, or St. Francis, in the vogue of Sabatier's books, or Joergensen's, or Aristotle, in neo-scholasticism, or, whether His Resurrection, being what tradition says it was, set a unique seal on a career and doctrine themselves unique. It matters, if baptism imparts a substantial supernatural life, or is a social function, or at best a signification of a call to ethical improvement. The Pharisees, nay, the first Apostles, had plenty of conscience. Our Lord tried to instruct them, and failed with the former, but succeeded with the Twelve.

Nor did Christ make us over to a book, inspired or not. He wrote no book, nor foreboded any; nor did His followers suggest any such thing, nor was Church founded on New Testament, but New Testament was a product of a Church; nor is there reason for judging that the New Testament, let alone the Old, has an absolutely authoritative voice, save if some other duly accredited voice shall authoritatively tell us so. What of its intrinsic persuasiveness? This can but persuade us of that very fact—that it is persuasive, as Plato may be, or Dante; but even if successive generations have agreed about the persuasiveness of parts of it, they have not done so with regard, say, to the epistle of Jude, the book of Numbers, the story of Esther, or even much of St. Paul. Indeed, if we make the inspiredness of the Bible to rest on its inspiringness, we shall not get far, nor for long. Nor can we make a compromise, and say that the Church (whatever that may prove to be) has the right to teach us what the Bible means, provided it never steps outside it, for the Church's very first business would have to be, and indeed was soon enough seen to be, to tell us what *is* "Bible". That is an extra-Biblical piece of information: neither Testament gives any hint on the subject. Nor even have groups of consciences—non-infallible "denominations"—the right to offer more than that relative cogency that any good man may provide, and, while we respect such an one, we sit quite lightly to what he tells us. We fear that nowadays this is quite off the point: men sample the Bible, when not just criticizing it; take what serves them; leave or correct what displeases them; and do the same, really, to Christ Himself. They equivalently say: "We respect Him, but, by now we have learnt better." From what we have said, we see that Christ was able to found an infallibly teaching society if He wished to: He had the right to; and He had reasons for wishing to. And from the New Testament documents regarded (as they ought to be) as massively reliable, even though not yet as inspired, so that no vicious circle is implied, we hold that He actually did so.

We certainly do not propose to set down the whole "apologetic" of the Christian Church, but only enough to enable a reader to know what is at the back of the Catholic mind when a Catholic thinks of the Church as "founded by Christ". Within a floating mass of Christ's hearers, a rather vaguely defined group of "disciples" formed itself. From these He chose twelve—"The Twelve" —whom He called Apostles, and sent them "as" His

Father had sent Him, to teach the whole world, and to
do so under a guarantee, so that those who should hear
them, would be hearing Him, as those who heard Him,
were hearing God. Similarly, to "despise" an Apostle,
would be to despise God. The series is exact: God, Christ,
the Apostles, the latter being mouthpiece and representative of the former. Moreover, they were to govern under
a like guarantee: what they should "loose", allow, or
"bind", forbid, on earth, should be ratified in heaven,
by God. Here indeed is a good implicit statement of
what the Catholic means by infallibility. The Apostles
would *not* be able to teach a lie or command in Christ's
name a sin, else they would involve God Himself. But
since no man can thus exempt himself from the fate of
human frailty, they were safeguarded by God Himself
from failing in their office. The favour belonged to the
office, not to the person. And so the Apostles conceived
of themselves. "It has been decided by the Holy Ghost
and by Us" is the astounding preface to their first decree.
And without a break the Church thought of herself as
continuing this teaching office and function: her very
name was "The Teaching", and was opposed to that
Gnostic theory which was, that special and private
illumination gave to an élite the true knowledge of God.
Christianity is *not* a Gnosis, but a Didaché. The Church
has always been a Teaching Body, under the full guarantee
of Christ, and not a mere assembly of persons experiencing
emotions however noble or hatching ideas however
valuable and, in the last resort, governing themselves by
these.

Into this "closed system" there was one door: Faith
and Baptism; and out of it was to be one door; con-
tumacious rebellion and excommunication. Nor into the
Apostolic group could you insert yourself at will: Christ
chose the Twelve: the Twelve appointed their successors

and ever were to: never was it supposed that the Teaching
Office was diffused haphazard through the Church; the
Apostles themselves had to coerce the wandering "prophet". And among the Twelve, Christ gave to Simon
son of Jonas a special post. He changed his name to
Peter, not at random, but because he was to possess the
character, and fulfil the function, of a Rock, which Peter
means. Such ever was the point of the addition of a
surname to a Hebrew, to mention no others. After a
long space Christ showed why He had done this. He
asked the assembled Apostles whom men said He was.
"Some say one thing, some another." "Whom say *ye*?"
They were silent. Then Peter made his tremendous
affirmation. And Christ answered it with His own. "Oh,
the blessings that are thine! No human wits, nor instruction, have revealed that to thee, but God. And I say to
thee that thou art 'Rock', and upon this Rock will I
build My Church, and the Gates of Hell (that is, opposing
forces of destruction) shall never prevail against it."
Precisely because it was founded upon a God-guaranteed
Rock, it should never fall, as the Apostles, familiar with
Christ's tale of the Two Houses, very well understood.
Shift the building off that Rock, and there is no option
save the quicksand. And note, it is, quite simply, *the
Church* that is to stand upon that Rock. Permanent the
Church is; permanent must be Peter. The man was not
immortal, but his function and office are enduring. "And
to thee will I give the Keys of the Kingdom of Heaven."
The vivid picture of the Keys has eclipsed for many the
astounding words that follow. For a Hebrew, the com-
mittal of "keys" to a man meant the entrusting to him
complete control of all that was in chest, or house, or
town. Over what, then, was Peter for ever to have control?
Over that whole thing that Christ came to create, in so
far as it was on earth—The Kingdom of Heaven. Far

from this prerogative having been expanded by Catholic
centuries, you might say that the Church's definitions
have more accurately narrowed it. Christ could not
transfer His personal Messiahship to Peter, but He did
transfer thus two of its immemorial titles, the Rock, and
the Key-bearer: and Peter stands firm and for ever the
delegate and representative of God's own representative
and delegate to the world. Were not the Apostles, from
among whom he was chosen, exempt from this subordination? Certainly not. "Satan hath desired to have *you*,
to sift, scatter you like so many grains of wheat; but I
have prayed for *thee*, that *thy* faith fail not." And Peter's
office thereafter was to be one that gave cohesion and
stability to his very brethren. Finally, after the Resurrection, Christ transfers His full Messianic Shepherdhood
to Peter, and the more John's gospel be recognized as a
doctrinal one, the less can we rob those sentences of
their dogmatic value. We may note that so definite has
been the swing-back of criticism towards the traditional
significance of these words, being indeed the true one,
that those who are determined that Christ shall have
given no such prerogative to Peter, fly now to the deplor-
able *échappatoire* of interpolation, even in Matthew, "in
favour of the pretensions of the See of Rome". As if
so purely Palestinian a sentence could have been invented
in Rome, let alone successfully inserted into the most
Palestinian of gospels!

Henceforward, every item of evidence conspires with
what we have said, and none excludes or even militates
against it. At the so-called Council of Jerusalem, it is
Peter's dogmatic declaration that settles the question:
James, afterwards, appends some suggestions for a
practical application of Peter's ruling. Though not a
Council, this assembly followed a procedure almost
quaintly like that of an ecclesiastical council later on.

We may be positively grateful for the incident when Paul
so austerely rebuked Peter, who had failed in his personal
behaviour to act according to the implications of his
declared doctrine (just as Paul did himself afterwards,
from motives of expediency, when he caused Timothy
to be circumcised), so clearly does the story differentiate
between official rulings and individual action. Indeed,
such is the authority recognized by Paul to lodge in
Peter, that he fears lest the whole of his own converts
be morally "forced" to imitate Peter. Whether or no
Paul was right in judging Peter's action to be inexpedient,
his own, later on, to be expedient, who at this distance
shall decide? It remains that no principle was substantially tampered with on this side or on that.

We take it that the sojourn of Peter in Rome as its
bishop is now admitted. And whenever Rome or the
occupant of its see henceforward comes into play, it is
always as authoritative. Such certainly is the action of
Clement as to Corinth, a place not under his jurisdiction
(nay, under the very eye of the surviving Apostle John)
unless indeed his jurisdiction were conceived as general.
Victor, a hundred years later, is found preparing to excommunicate the bishops of the whole of Asia, not even in
his half of the world, since he discerned in their proposal
to celebrate a national Easter, the germ of the creation
of a "national church", as we should now say. Men
interceded with Victor, but none denied his right. For
a special reason we add, that when Irenæus suggests an
appeal to Rome "with which it is necessary that all
churches should agree", it is idle to dispute about the
possible meanings of each word, or their original, since
the whole point of his argument disappears—it is, against
Gnostic impressionism, that the Church is authoritative
in her official, episcopal teaching—if you suppose that
recourse is to be had to Rome for anything save

authoritative lessoning. Impossible to make him mean, "Go to Rome: everyone sooner or later has to go there: in Rome you will find witnesses from everywhere." As if "churches" could be described as pilgrimaging to Rome! Individuals might: the local church remained solidly seated. And as if the mere influx of all sorts of people would create a homogeneous opinion, and not rather conflict and chaos. And as if, anyhow, Irenæus cared anything for public opinion in such circumstances: no more than for private illuminism.

We pass soon enough into the period of the Great Councils, and, to our mind, this and the earliest period of all, that of the gospels, display the Petrine prerogative in process of defining its function more clearly than any other, and, we may add, more richly than the development of many another dogma, that, for example, which concerns the Holy Ghost, which for very long was relatively obscure. But we hold that without the double doctrine of the Infallibility of the Church and of Rome, the history of the Councils is barely intelligible. One could not see what *is* a "General" Council, nor even why it should bind the Church authoritatively. The Councils were not composed of a majority of the bishops: nor geographically representative; nor were they committees of very learned or even of very good men. Certainly they never dreamt that their decisions carried weight because the Christian folk would forthwith, or eventually, ratify them. The Christian folk had to obey their rulings, or go into schism. Nor did the bishops resort to them having collected the views of their constituents, so to say, meekly representing their diocesans. They went to make quite sure what the traditional faith was, chiefly in view of some dispute; to ascertain the best formula in which to express this; to get their conclusions ratified, and to impose them under pain of anathema. By what right did they claim to do this? because they claimed to teach in the name of the Church. All, in the Church, that *could* teach, taught in them. It is at once clear that they could not do this apart from, still less in defiance of, Rome, if only because all now admit that Rome held at least some sort of primacy in the Church. It became clear that the ideal Council would be one actually convened by, headed by, and ratified by the Pope. Then, manifestly, no such separation or defiance would exist. But each of these actions admits of "more or less": a Pope could, indeed can, approve of the summoning of a Council by the initiative of another, be that other an emperor, a metropolitan, or even a heretic: he might preside, and did, in the person of his legates; his acceptance, or acting upon, the Council's rulings, could count as ratification. But it will be found that all these elements exist in germ at least in the history of each Council. The notion of ratification is well expressed by Innocent I, January 417, when he applauded the African bishops for referring their local decisions to Rome, since they had but observed the immemorial practice, he said, which had its origin in no mere human arrangement, but by divine decree, "that nothing whatsoever, even if it concerned the uttermost parts of the earth, should be held fit to be decided till it had come to the knowledge of the Apostolic See", so that thus a just decree might be confirmed with the full authority of Rome, and that "the rest of the Churches" might learn thence "what to teach, whom to absolve, whom to reject as beyond cleansing", and thus "every stream" would be found to "proceed from its native fount, and the pure waters of an untainted source would percolate through every part of the entire world". I think it was Zosimus, in 418, quickly followed by Boniface I, in 422, who inaugurated the formula: "There can be no going back upon our verdict. For never has

it been permitted that what has once been settled by the
Apostolic See, should enter again into controversy."

The Councils of Ephesus and of Chalkedon display
the papal function operating to its full extent, and are
ideal evidence of the sort we seek from history as to the
early state of a dogma. Celestine must definitely be
regarded as having sent Cyril of Alexandria to Ephesus,
if not technically as his legate at least as his representative, bidding him add to the authority of Alexandria the
"full authority" of the Holy See, and, telling him what
the Council was to decide, and within what time. When
the legates in fact arrived, Philip said: "No one calls
in question, nay, rather has it been admitted by all ages,
that the holy and most blessed Peter, exarch and head
of the Apostles, the pillar of the Faith, the foundation
of the Catholic Church, received from our Lord Jesus
Christ, the Saviour, the Keys of the Kingdom. . . .
Peter, who till to-day, and for ever, both lives and teaches
in the person of his successors."

And Chalkedon's oriental prelates well said to Leo,
along with much enthusiastic homage, that in the person
of his representatives he not only demonstrated the right
doctrine, but presided as a head presides over limbs. I
have no doubt but that they mean to express that organic
relation in which the Pope stands to the Church as a
whole, and I can think of few more feeble considerations
than to ascribe to meaningless flattery sentences which
after all do mean something quite intelligible.

We have quoted these two incidents, though we do
not think that the papal position is best dealt with by
means of isolated utterances, however conclusive, just as
it is in no sense injured by instances of revolt.[1] The

---

[1] For a popular discussion of the Councils (for even this we are not
making here), including that of Nicæa, cf. Dom. J. Chapman's *Church and
the Councils.*

latter can all be explained by the circumstances, the former cannot be explained save by a consistent tradition. Still less should a local or political origin be sought for the papal power. Had not the Pope been intrinsically what he claimed, not only the Churchman-Pharaoh at Alexandria, or the bishop of New Rome, but the very bishops of Milan and even Ravenna, I should say, would soon enough have eclipsed that dweller in a grass-grown city. And no one more consistently cut his own throat politically than did the Roman bishop, who approved of corn-supplying Alexandria, and imperially flamboyant Constantinople just so long as they taught true doctrine, only to turn and smite them with his thunderbolts the moment they did not.

The papal rule seems to us, in this period, to emerge best as follows. Everyone admitted that the Church could teach no error. Everyone admitted too that Rome was the final Court of Appeal. You could not go back upon Rome's decisions: therefore, what Rome decided was the doctrine of the Church, and true. We do not insist on the else curious fact that Rome, a practical place, not strong in abstract theology, and having laboriously to create some sort of language in which to express herself, which in itself was enough to exasperate a Greek, should yet invariably have managed to state what anyone now can see to be the true consequences of doctrine as hitherto taught. We do not believe in happy flukes, repeated over and over again, when to make one even once was improbable. We suppose that instances of Popes teaching the Church a wrong doctrine are rarely urged to-day. The case of Honorius used to intrigue students, if only because he was condemned of personal heresy, a fault of which he or any Pope could of course be guilty. No one who begins to understand the doctrine of papal infallibility will begin to suppose that Honorius

taught error to the Church. In fact, Honorius was right
in all he said, though he might have said more than he
said, and officially. But as we shall insist, infallibility
is not inspiration, nor omniscience, nor even prudence.

No. We like here as everywhere else to watch the
gradual development of the living Church. An organism
need not so much as look, at first, very like what it will
become. But all of it is there. It will use and misuse and
fail to use and even be unable to use all its limbs, or all
of them equally or any of them perfectly: it is by trying
that it finds out in detail what it can do or can't, and
even what it is meant to do. A baby has its bones and
muscles, yet it cannot walk. It kicks idly; it totters.
But by experiment, function is not only developed, but
revealed. Last of all, the baby will theorize about itself,
or someone else will for it. It will decide that there are
useless kicks, and vicious kicks, and honest perambula-
tion. In the end, it may become a scientific man who can
make charts of the human frame and assign the extent
of its powers, and their nature, with accuracy. It is easy,
then, in looking back, to see how perfect the Church's
organism always was. Pope, bishops, clergy, faithful—
all were there. Yet not so easy, for a time, to know just
what could be done by each, legitimately, wisely, or at all.
Even now, perhaps, the absolutely exact relation of the
Pope to bishops, or collectivities of bishops, may not
have been exhaustively defined, though for practical purposes it has been. But life always triumphs. There was
a double law of life for Peter's successor: he must exist,
by Christ's institution, a bishop among, and over, bishops:
and he cannot, as such, teach the Church a doctrine other
than Christ's own. From this simple law—a "law", for
once, in both senses—all further development has come.

The doctrine of the Vatican Council about this is
that:

(1) Christ willed to found a Church wherein all the Faithful should be contained as in one house. He willed that in this Church there should be shepherds and teachers. And that the episcopate should be one and undivided, and that the Faithful should be preserved in unity of faith and communion, he set Peter over the rest of the Apostles and constituted in his person the perpetual principle and visible foundation of "both unities": that is, of the hierarchy, and of the people. And again,

(2) Our Lord gave to Peter immediately and directly a primacy of jurisdiction over the entire Church, so that it is false to say that it is the Church or anyone in her who gave Peter his position as though he were her minister and appointment. Hence—

(3) This primacy of jurisdiction is also permanent, and endures in Peter's successors, so that he who sits in Peter's Chair and because he sits there, obtains the prerogative proper to Peter's office.

(4) Hence the Roman Pontiff is the successor of Peter, true Vicar of Christ, head of the entire Church, and father and teacher of all Christians, and has full jurisdiction over all the Faithful of whatsoever Rite, and has therefore authority not only in what concerns the declaration of Faith and Morals, but in matters of discipline and government, though this is so far from interfering with the ordinary jurisdiction of bishops (who hold their authority direct from Christ) that it asserts, corroborates, and sanctions that jurisdiction. Hence he who should declare that the Bishop of Rome has but an inspectional or directive office, and not full and supreme power over the whole Church in these departments, or has but a priority of rank, or some sort of extraordinary or mediate authority, is to be condemned.

(5) It is, to conclude, defined that "the Roman Pontiff, when he speaks *ex cathedra* (that is, when, fulfilling his

function as pastor and teacher of all Christians, in the name of his supreme apostolic authority he defines a doctrine concerning faith or morals as to be held by the universal Church), by the divine assistance promised to him in Blessed Peter possesses that infallibility with which the Divine Redeemer willed His Church to be equipped in the defining of faith or morals, and therefore, the definitions of the said Roman Pontiff are irreformable of their own nature and not owing to the consent of the Church".

We hope we have made the facts clear. The infallibility of the Pope does not mean that he is impeccable, nor omniscient, nor inspired. He may be privately a heretic; he may wish to teach false doctrine; he may not know what the true doctrine about a matter so far undefined may be. The one thing he cannot do is to teach false doctrine, as Pope, to the Universal Church. He cannot turn from rock to sand: he cannot pull the columns of the Church apart; he cannot feed the flock on poison. His charism of infallibility is a negative one; and whatsoever Providence may guide his behaviour or policy, whatsoever private inspirations he may receive, these are outside the notion of infallibility. How grotesque, then, are criticisms such as that this Pope or that did not, or does not, define a doctrine when the critic judges it is needed. Perhaps the Pope played false to his trust: perhaps at the time he could not define a dogma without presumption; perhaps it would have been against prudent charity to define it, as it would, were a definition calculated to send more souls into schism than non-definition would leave souls in hesitation. How off the point, too, is the suggestion that there are two infallibilities, if not three—Church at large, Council, and Pope. There is but one infallibility, Christ's; and Christ, organically united with the Church, His Body, communicates to her His infallibility, and with *that* infallibility the Pope, as visible head of the Church, is equipped. The whole thing is organic, and not the result of human negotiation. Observe that this is no minimizing of the dogma: it is exactly what the Vatican defined.

But there is small satisfaction to be derived from this by those who would maintain that somehow Christian groups out of union with the Sovereign Pontiff form a structural part of the Church. Individuals within them may well be, as we shall say, in God's Grace: but form part of the Church of Christ as by Him established, they do not. Since the Roman Church teaches what we have just said, it follows that either Roman Catholics are heretics, or those who teach the opposite to them, namely, that you need *not* be in union with the Pope, are heretics. An unbridged gulf has been cleft. The possession of Orders has nothing to do with the matter: whether or no the entire faith other than this dogma be taught by such groups, again makes no matter. Suppose an individual belonging to such a group believes even the dogma of papal infallibility, as some are incomprehensibly said to do, that does not set him within the Church, any more than to agree that some officer was Generalissimo of the Allied Armies would make a man a member of that army or of any other. Nor would it justify a man in doing the very first thing that the Pope, whose authority he professes to acknowledge, would forbid, namely, to stay where he is. To remain in a group alien from Rome, so as to modify it in a Roman direction, would be like a Jew refusing baptism, that he might guide the Synagogue Church-wards; for an Arian to refuse to sign the Nicene creed, though he had come to believe in it, that he might improve the Arian heresy from inside; for a woman to live with a man not her husband in the hopes of effecting a marriage some day, and meanwhile to prevent him

from wandering sin. If the Pope would refuse Communion to one who denied this dogma, so would he to
one who admitted it but refrained from its concrete
consequences. There is here no particularly English view,
but a natural and necessary application of a principle;
and the difference between the clearness with which, for
example, an English ecclesiastic can see the situation,
and that with which a foreign one can, is due entirely
to the Latin intelligence failing to admit as conceivable
those vaguenesses and illogical confusions that are so
congenial to the northern mind.

This section of our book may have seemed unsympathetic. It was not really so. We have wished to put
clearly forth a dogma with its implications. It was a
skeleton: skeletons do not excite sympathy or the reverse.
What we feel for a living person is a different matter.
Different too is the extent to which a Catholic may
habitually or at a crisis exult in, chafe under, humbly and
gratefully obey, or revolt against the authority of the
Roman See. This is an affair of personal virtue or temperament or both. Most Catholics experience in the
matter no problem at all. They are at home in their
Father's house; they love and are proud of their Pope.
They think of him *as* their Father, as indeed he is, having
never hidden behind silk curtains like who knows what
mysterious Caliph, Shah, or Sultan. It is part of that
general faith, trust, and affection, that they preserve
themselves quite at peace even should they not understand all his motives. Why should they? What subordinate ever expects to know the complete mind of his
ruler? Of course they expect to be asked, and are proud
to be asked, at times, for sacrifices, or to receive irksome
commands, as not to become a freemason; or, like the
French clergy a generation ago, to sacrifice their entire
means of support; or, what bites more deeply, though

it is concerned with the nature of things and not an affair of policy, to forgo all methods of birth-restriction. They may be naughty—in what family are there not naughty children? One hopes they will "grow better". They may sulk; or howl; or try and fail and try again —will do all that men do who live under authority. But they will judge themselves, and expect to *be* judged, or checked, as when forbidden to use certain formulas, or to adhere to certain unproved theories; or to read or succumb to a certain book. Let no one cheaply think that it is always easy to obey authority; or, that because it is difficult, a man must doubt, or condemn authority; or, that because he obeys a subordinate authority that may even be wrong, he regards himself as a slave. Life is far larger than all that, and Life always wins.

A brief question. Does not this interfere with the advance of science and scholarship? It doesn't: but if once in a way it did, we should not much mind. Assume (for argument's sake) that Catholics were once forbidden to teach that the "Comma Iohanneum" was an interpolation. They always knew that decision was not infallible: they are now free in the matter. But suppose they still were bound. What would it matter? Do we even base our belief in the Trinity on that text? Of course not. And has that veto interfered with Scriptural study among Catholics? Equally of course not. It was never so keen as now. Looking back, one can see how valuable have such checks been. From how many a fashion, or fad, of the moment have students not been saved! Imagine if we had succumbed to the Tübingen school when it tried to date the gospels: or the Dutch school, when it talked about St. Paul. Not only are Catholics watching critics come round to positions abandoned fifty years ago, but they have learnt themselves to support with better reasons than what, without attack,

they would have troubled to seek out, the "orthodox"
positions. The Church is extremely patient and has
excellent nerves. She often says: "Wait: do not lose your
head. Do not jump to conclusions. Don't, please, have
hysterics. At present you can't say what you want to.
Perhaps you may later on; perhaps, later on, you won't
even want to. Least of all can you say your new idea
is demonstrated. You must even try to think respectfully
of the opposite idea. You will be glad, some day, scientifi-
cally: you can be glad, at once, religiously. God help
us! our affair is Eternity: we are not going to risk that
for a detail of scholarship."

We add, that it is extremely unlikely that anyone not
trained in the very technical language of Roman congre-
gations, will be able to interpret them properly. Some
time ago we read a long article, meant to be wholly fair,
on the decrees of the Biblical Commission. We think
that every single one of its comments contained an
inaccuracy or even a grave error of interpretation.[1]

[1] Though to set down the Church's *doctrine* on any subject is here to
anticipate what properly belongs to the second half of the book, it may
be better to state what she teaches about Scripture. Scripture, as we saw,
is the product of the Church, not her origin. She does not draw her
doctrine from the Bible, but that which the Bible teaches will necessarily
be Catholic doctrine and therefore can in many ways be used to illustrate
it, and even to "prove" it in the sense of showing that dogma is not at
variance with the doctrine of the first Christian generation. In a word,
the Scriptures, regarded (as I hold we ought to regard them) as reliable
historical documents, show us that Christ, able to do so, instituted an
infallibly teaching Church. That Church in her turn teaches us facts about
the Scriptures that we could not else have known. The supremely important fact is that they are inspired. Other documents *may* have been inspired,
but we have no knowledge of it. By inspiration, we mean this at least—
God moved the writer to write, so that God is as much responsible for
the consequences as the human author is. In one sense the document will
be wholly from God, in another wholly from the writer. This implies that
such documents are inerrant (a consequence of inspiration, but not inspiration itself). Therefore, what the writer means to say, will be true.
Now, you can mean to say, and say, a thing in many different ways. A
chronicler of the war, a war-novelist, a poet, a cartoonist, a blue-book,
record the story of the Great War each in his own way. Allow that each
tells the truth: none the less, the *way* of telling truthfully the same fact

Is, then, the Church a cruel exclusivist? a chill administrator of ecclesiastical snubs? Not more so than Christ and His Apostles were, but just so much as they. If a man believes all Catholic doctrine, and then stays outside the Church, alas for him. "But it must similarly be held for certain" (wrote Pius IX, December 9, 1854), "that they who suffer from real ignorance of religion, if they cannot conquer it, are not bound by any fault herein before the eyes of the Lord. And now who will arrogate to himself so much as to think he can define the limits of such ignorance, according to the nature and variety of peoples, places, temperaments, and so many

---

will differ in each case. When God "moves" a statistician, a mystic, a moralist, a (shall I say) fictionist, to write, it is *that man* whom He so moves, and each man will write wholly in the way that is congenial to him. Neither grammar, syntax, vocabulary, nor habitual choice of literary vehicle will be interfered with. There is no *a priori* objection to inspired fiction. *Esther* may be that. So may *Tobias*. But what the inspired author asserts will be true. Before you know what he does assert, it is your business to make sure in what *way* he is asserting it. I shall recall, below, that if a historian says: "The king of Babylon defeated the king of Juda": and if a prophet says: "A lion came out of the north and devoured My gazelle"; each is asserting exactly the same thing. The second statement is infallibly true, even though there were no lion and no gazelle. The detailed discussion of instances belongs entirely to critics: if they are Catholic critics, they know that what God's Spirit inspired and taught in Scripture, cannot conflict with what the same Spirit teaches through the Church. We add, that inspiration is not the same as, though it may be coupled with, revelation. If a plodding examiner of documents or traditions be inspired to write, ploddingly will he examine his favourite material. So presumably, St. Luke. St. John, in his gospel, would have consulted chiefly his own memories; in the Apocalypse (for we hold that there are no reasons, exterior or internal, sufficient to prove that the two documents were not written by the same man: indeed, we hold that there are sound reasons—sound, precisely because subtle—for holding that the author was in each case the son of Zebedee) there may well have been a full element of revelation too. Hence the Church claims that she, who informed us of what is Scripture, and of what Scripture is, also has the right, and alone possesses the right, to tell us what Scripture means. In a word; the Church it is to whom Christ has given the right and the duty of teaching; part of her teaching is the "topic" of Scripture; and since the One Spirit cannot teach or cause to be taught Contradictories, what Scripture asserts will be what the Church asserts, though it never need be all that the Church asserts.

other things? For when we are freed from the captivity
of the body and see God as He is, we shall forthwith
understand by what close and beautiful bonds are bound
together the divine mercy and the divine justice: so long
as we live here on earth, weighed down by this mortal
flesh, that dulls the soul, let us most firmly hold that
according to Catholic doctrine there is one God, one
Faith, one Baptism, and to go further [in our inquiry as
to the fate of souls] were sin."

Our Reason, then, playing upon the nature of God,
and of man, can lead us so far as this tenderness that is
not complaisance, but is just and indeed inevitable. When
we speak of God's Grace, we shall find further reason
for contentment. We have then so far set forth the substratum of Catholic doctrine—our belief in God, and the
soul, and in its vocation to eternal happiness by way of
right intelligent choice; belief in the Revelation of God
given uniquely and finally to man by Jesus Christ; belief
that Christ founded a Church for the safe perpetuation
of that revelation; a Church with a definite structure,
an essential element in which is Peter, who lives and
rules in the person of the Roman Pontiffs his successors.
On those who know this, rests the grave obligation to put
themselves in organic contact with that Church, and to
believe what she teaches and to do what she orders.
Having ascertained that she teaches Truth and can teach
nothing else, we could, indeed, just accept in the mass
what she does so teach, since it must be true. But this
indolent path must be eschewed, and we ought to see
in detail what her doctrine is, as we shall now do, that
we may make our choices with more intelligence and
courage. And it can now be seen that by faith in general
I mean the intellectual assent given to a proposition, as
true, set before me by one whom I have reason to regard
as an adequate authority: by faith, in the sense in which

this book concerns itself with it, I mean the accepting as God's Truth a proposition set forth to me by that Authority which, I have reason to believe, is guaranteed by God to teach me, and because it is thus guaranteed.

PART II

CATHOLIC DOCTRINE

1. The Most Blessed Trinity

A T THE head of the Church's doctrine is the dogma
of GOD, One and Three. All that reason has been
able to tell us about Him, the Church reinforces. But
while we could know, without revelation, that His will
is all-good and therefore good to us, and though we could
thus "love" Him with many kinds of love, like that of
"preference" so that we chose Him before all things else,
and of gratitude, and indeed with a just and profound
emotion, yet our Lord has bidden us concentrate more
than else we might have upon that lovableness of God.
We are right to use every human analogue, as of Father-
hood, to help us to penetrate more deeply the fact of
His loving us. We are right to give priority to the thought
that God *is* Love, and loves us. For love elicits love;
and one way of thinking about Christianity is that it is
God's way of making us love Him perfectly, and thus to
grow like Him, be united with Him, and happy in Him,
eternally.

But the Catholic Faith teaches that this God, whom
all own to be One with a unity that exceeds all that we
can humanly intend by that word, is also truly Three.
The Scripture illustrates this not only in the great Bap-
tismal formula, but constantly. The unique and reciprocal
knowledge of the Father and the Son (Matt. xi. 27) is
founded on an identity of Being stated beyond doubt by
John and by Paul. In the One God, Father is other than
Son, and Son than Father. And certainly the Scriptures

present the Spirit as true God: yet He too is other than Father and than Son, and proceeds from and is sent by Each. Theology almost at once rejected the view that the Three were but "aspects" of the One and owed their very existence, as Three, to our human minds, and the word Person was chosen to help us to think and to speak of Them aright. We recall that whatever limitation the word "person", as humanly used among ourselves, may import, we exclude when speaking of God. We assert that the perfections that constitute Personality exist in God infinitely and as in their source, and are verified triply in the One God who is Father, Son, and Spirit.

This is the supreme instance of what we have called a "Mystery". A mystery is a truth whereof we need to be told even its possibility, let alone that it exists. It totally transcends in essence any power of discovery that is ours. But not for that is it useless to us; still less, without meaning. We can quite well see what is meant by: God is One. And that Father, Son, and Spirit are each True God. The "how" of this we certainly cannot grasp, though many a shadowy analogue has been offered to thought. Memory, for example, intellect, and will; for no one of these is either of the others, and yet each is the whole soul. And human nature exhausts itself neither in the male nor in the female, but requires two persons to fulfil its reality; and indeed, these two unite in expressing themselves in the child, so that the true human unit, the family, is provided.

Nor dare we say that the revelation of this or any other mystery is not "useful". You may see with what joy and indeed rapture the Saints have contemplated it, and the simplest can share in that joy. We have hinted what the thought of God our Father can mean to the soul: what the Son may mean, we shall see: read but the Acts, or St. Paul, to guess what a power of life is in our belief in the Holy Spirit. From the summit of the Holy City, where God's Throne is set within the very source of Light, the Holy Spirit steals forth and then proceeds cascading down the terraced jewel-bright slopes of the new Mount Zion, by streets of translucent gold, giving life to that Grove of Life whose very leaves are for the healing of the nations. Always the Spirit has been the river whose rush makes glad God's City; and the ancient hymns, *Veni Creator*, *Veni Sancte*, may infuse into our hearts something of that peace and power that triumphed in those who long ago composed them.

But more. Conceivably the thought of God, One and Immutable, generates in us the illusion that He is inert, static merely. We can make ourselves see that His Life is one of unimaginable intensity, and be grateful to science for showing us the incredible energy latent in the minimum of created things. For this makes it ever easier for us to think of God, our Creator and Preserver, in terms of Activity and Force. But the Trinity reveals to us, if we dare so put it, a manifold Life in the 'solitude' of God. The Eternal Father knows His own Self, and generates thus His subsistent Thought, His immanent Word, His Divine Wisdom. There is here then a certain Relation as between Two, and, since in God nothing can be less than Infinite Reality, the Term of this relation must be as Personal as its eternal Generator: therefore, too, there passes (we still speak with the folly of human thought playing on the divine) between the Two an infinite and no less personal Love, and, if we like, we can speak of the Third in that Trinity *as* Love. There is then a Society in the One God; as it were a Familyhood, from likeness to which, as St. Paul says, all familyhood on earth wins its name (Eph. iii. 15); and from this fact much flows that is of value on unlooked-for levels. For from the Trinity we can gain our purest idea, for example, of

Peace, which means a state wherein can be the maximum of harmonious action; and wisely will a man, who seeks to govern persons or even nations, recall that in God's perfect Unity there has been no suppression of this or of that, nor fusion merely. Even at this hour, there are nations that try to tyrannize over their weaker elements, or to merge them into the stronger. Idly, for the Perfect Truth should find its reflection on any level of reality whatsoever.

2. MAN AND THE SUPERNATURAL LIFE

God created all that is. What He made was good, and each part was meant to achieve the perfection suited to it, and so to give Him Glory. Negatively imperfect then as the world, being finite, needs must be, there was in it no element and no tendency that were bad. And in the world was life, animal and sensitive life, vegetative life and human life; and the last differed from the rest, being intelligent and free.[1]

[1] What must Catholics hold about the creation of Man ? what are they free to surmise? where are they checked ? They hold, on grounds of reason, and also because the Church teaches it, that the human soul is "spirit", in essence different from "matter", and cannot "grow out of it" whatever that may mean, nor can matter "turn into" spirit, any more than the paints can turn into the artist's vision. And a spirit, being "simple" and partless, cannot emerge from, split off from, be generated by, another. Hence each spirit, angelic or human, has to be created by God; and since there is not one soul in all of us, each human soul has been created by God. But "man" is the union of matter and spirit in a complex unity, a complete substance, into a "person". Men are not now said to be created, because though their spiritual coefficient needs to be created and "infused" into its material coefficient, the latter has been transmitted by and from human parents. But when God first created a spirit meant to be united with matter and did so unite it, Man sprang into being and "man" was thus "created". The Church does not teach the method, but the fact of this creation. Do we, however, know it ? Certainly no philosophical prejudgment, nor fear of introducing "miracle", still less any evidence supplied by anthropologists, prevents us from saying that God immediately created or disposed the matter that was united with the first "human" spirit so as to form the first man. He may have done so. But Catholic dogma does not prevent a student from surmising that God

Here we must state a dogma of the Catholic Faith that must at all costs be understood if what follows is to be understood. It is that God freely willed to give to human

---

infused the spirit into matter already existing, already organized, already alive. There neither is, nor can be, evidence to show that He did; it may seem symmetrical and otherwise attractive to suppose that He did; or on other grounds improbable that He did: but here the Church has defined nothing. Catholic thinkers, in days before the problem was set before them, naturally did not hatch the notion that He did; but their principles of thought would not have excluded the notion that He had done so, and sometimes they led up to it. But recall always that even if God created and then infused the first "soul" into a *living creature*, that creature was not "human body" until God had done so: it was not even engaged in becoming human body; and even if God did so, the human body could not be described as having had animal ancestry. To talk about days when "we" were monkeys (or some such thing) would still be quite meaningless. The creation and infusion of "soul" are instantaneous actions, and so, in consequence, was the apparition of "human body". A Catholic cannot then use the fluid term Evolution as implying that non-human animals somehow turned without special act of God into human, nor that non-human parents somehow, still without that special act, produced a human. It is moreover involved in Catholic doctrine that there *was* a first human "pair", and that man did not "spring up" simultaneously or successively all over the world surface. The Church then defines that God created man, as we have said; but does not define whether He used for that, existing, organized, living matter, or did not. Nor can the relics that anthropology exhibits prove anything whatsoever except that man's body was always more or less like non-human bodies, which no one is tempted, I suppose, to doubt. Creation is not an affair for research, but of philosophy and dogma. As for the Scriptures, we have said above that the Church defines them to be inspired, and hence, inerrant, so that what the writer means to assert is true. We here repeat that a historian, a poet, a mystic, a moralist, will probably assert different orders of facts, and even the same facts in different ways. Probably every "sort" of literature can be found within the inspired writings. As for the narratives concerning the Creation, we know that the writer means to assert historical facts, and that none of them conflicts with dogma. It remains to make sure what facts he asserts, and in what way, or ways. Many facts did the author manifestly mean to assert, e.g. that God created all things, even the stars (which were not lesser gods), and that, without having to fight an antagonistic chaos; that what He made was not evil in itself; that Man was created in a special manner, and that his nature is twofold—consisting, in one part, of the same elements as the rest of material creation, in the other, of that which makes him "in the image and likeness" of God, as a son is in his father's, and which can be described as "the breath of God". In the last words, I imply that metaphor can be looked for in these narratives, and of course the Church's official documents explicitly say the same. But my point is that a historical fact can well be stated metaphorically, as we daily see: cf. p. 60. The Church will naturally be very slow to allow us to *assert* that this or that *is* metaphor, if only because

nature a life that was superhuman. Take an illustration, though not a parallel. Imagine sensitive life being imparted to a stone: animal life to a flower. Why not a parallel? Because the gift of intellectual life, a spiritual soul, to a brute, would make it no more a brute at all. Its species would have been changed. But man being already "spiritual", will not be altered specifically by being "raised" to a supernatural way of existing. He will remain a man, though endowed with supernatural powers. We do not suppose that this sort of objection would occur spontaneously to most of those for whom

---

people who want to get rid of what worries them, will tend to introduce metaphor wantonly. But take an example. We are free to think that the author of Genesis i, being in possession of a seven-day week, and wishing to plot out the manifold creation of the world in a logical scheme, used the "week" as his framework. So far as there is a Catholic tradition on this point (there is no authoritative one), it would seem rather to be on the side of the simultaneous creation of all things in some sort of rich and inclusive cause, so that the aboriginal impulse, so to say, coupled of course with the divine preservation, sent the world forward on a line of change and elaboration. Certain Christian Fathers who, no one doubts, were fully "creationist", were prepared to admit the generation of animal life itself from inanimate matter. Augustine and Aquinas contemplate the possibility of simultaneous creation with perfect serenity; Anastasius II (under the influence obviously of Augustine) wrote in 498: " They should understand this too that is written: ' He that liveth for ever created all things simultaneously.' If, therefore, before the Scripture arranged an order and system in the several creatures by means of the several species, God (as cannot be denied) worked potentially and causally in the work that concerned creating all things simultaneously, etc." This would seem to be *not* an infallible pronouncement chiefly because the Pope was primarily speaking of something else, and asserting that souls were not physically handed down from parent to child. Hence, since the observer's eye could never, even to-day, diagnose the creation and infusion of a soul by God, we do not see how anthropological science can ever produce anything to clash with Catholic doctrine; as we said, all it can show is that man, however and whenever he came into being, did not do so in a world in which there was nothing else whatsoever physically at all like him. That, we always knew. All we are perhaps learning is, *what* else there was in the world when man so appeared. Strictly speaking, it seems that there is only one point at which Catholic dogma goes beyond the due philosophy of creation—that is, that the human race is descended from one original pair, and that there never will be "men" who have not descended from that pair. And this we learn, really, from our knowledge of other dogmas, chiefly that of Original Sin and Redemption.

we are writing, but we state it because it is almost impossible to make people realize that we mean something substantial and real by the Supernatural Life. They insist on thinking that it means "living holily", or heroically, if not spookily. We keep being told that to live supernaturally means living as we now do, only more so. An improvement of what we possess. No. Catholic doctrine does not mean merely an addition, as (assuming that N stands for "natural", S for "supernatural") the formula N plus S would signify: but still less does it mean a mere intensification, as N^n would signify. $N \times S$ would be much more nearly accurate. I think that the absolute fury which I have seen the Catholic doctrine of the Supernatural Life excite in quite sedate persons, is due to their being infected with the idea that there *must* be no "breaks" in existence, but that everything must develop equably into the next thing, a quite arbitrary and *a priori* notion, if indeed it has any meaning, which I doubt. Also, because so personal an intervention of God would involve terrific responsibilities; also, certain connected dogmas. These being distasteful to such persons, what leads up to them logically is at once withdrawn. Anyway, the Church teaches that humans are meant to possess a superhuman life, and to enjoy its consequences. What are these?

There are different "sorts" of knowledge. My friend knows me otherwise than my dog does: a flower, though "alive", does not know me at all. But upon knowledge love depends, and union with the beloved implies assimilation thereto, and reciprocity of life between the two, and joy accordingly. If, then, my soul be supernaturalized, it can know God, love Him, be united with and happy in and like to Him, supernaturally. What though the fruition of this be as it were inhibited, provided the root of the thing be there, which it is, if "grace" be present.

"We *have* Eternal Life." "We are called 'children of God' (instead of mere 'sons of men'), and so indeed we *are*." All that eternity stores up for us, beyond what Grace gives us, is the fixation of that Grace, and the full harmonization of all man with this supreme element within him, and his adequate consciousness of his supernatural life. At present, we claim no consciousness, we expect no evidential proof, of the existence of all this within us: we take it on faith, as the ancient Hebrews, whom St. Paul so praises, took on faith, even despite evidence, God's promise of their Messianic destiny.

But such a doctrine, they say, is dangerous. It shifts your centre of gravity. If you believe in this mystical future and indeed present, you neglect the "natural virtues" that should be cultivated by all decent folks. For the sake of a vision you sacrifice the obvious duty and decency. We admit the shifting, and we allow for the danger. We, too, insist that we have here no "abiding city", and that the pageant of this world is transient enough. We may even ache, with St. Paul, in our yearning to be disentangled from the shadow and the symbol, from the anguish of our fragmentary knowledge, seeing even God, as we do, "as by means of a mirror, dimly", and grow tired even of those high virtues—faith and its obscurity, hope and its "how long?" But we shall pray to be true to those daily sober virtues that Christ and His Apostles enjoin on us, and for one act of which St. Teresa said she would give all her ecstasies. Nor has the Church ever failed to keep the good balance. The hermit period, one might have thought, would have seen the eclipse of the "natural virtues". But read that sanest, shrewdest of books, the *Lausiac History of Palladius*. See what downright social forces were the great monastic founders, and remember that if at times the supernatural life of charity needs to be emphasized as against the mere life of ethics or philanthropy, less risk is being run by the Catholic who is so reminded, than disaster is incurred by the man who does not even know what you mean, if you mention "supernatural life"

3. THE TWO ADAMS

God, we are taught, gave this life to our first parents not forcing it on them, but humanwise, as an affair of choice, dependent on their obedience to a moral command proportionate to their knowledge of Him and of His will. They disobeyed it, lost thus their original "justice", and were forthwith deprived of their life of supernatural grace. This is the "Fall". The Fall, then, has to do with this deprivation of supernatural grace, and nothing directly to do with natural life at all. After the Fall, Adam and Eve were on exactly the same plane, in exactly the same conditions, naturally speaking, as before. True, God had also given them certain preternatural gifts which they would have retained had they retained their "grace", especially a harmony of their instincts with reason, and exemption from physical death: but these had nothing to do with the constituents of their nature as such, still less with their level of civilization. Of that we know nothing, save that the moment after the Fall, it was just as it was the moment before it. Dismiss, then, the caricature so often put forward, of the Fall—that Adam and Eve were on some exalted level of natural civilization, off which they fell. No doubt the withdrawal of supernatural grace and preternatural assistance left them to that limited human intelligence which so soon becomes darkened, and to those weaknesses that are inherent in human will, and to that rapidly aroused tumult of the instincts which we all experience: but these are echoes of the Fall, not the Fall itself.

But the race is not an aggregate of units. It is itself a unit and we exist in solidarity. In particular, we were summed up in the person of our first parent. Therefore, in him, the race was deprived of that supernatural life that should have been its privilege. A crude example. A king makes a man a duke. Should he commit treason he is deprived of his dukedom, and so are his heirs even though unborn. He commits that wrong: he is no more duke: nor will his descendants be. But he remains a man; so do they; no natural faculty of theirs is altered. So for us. Incorporate with Adam, we in him were deprived of that free gift of God's to him, and in him, to the race. This is the doctrine of Original Sin. Travesties of this too are set forth by persons ignorant of its history, and unable to look behind the versions re-afloat since the religious revolution of the sixteenth century. Original Sin is *not* an evil bias, a tendency to wrong, a taint in spirit or in flesh, a corruption of any part of human nature as such. "Concupiscence", the natural activity of instincts or passions not subordinate to reason, *is* not Original Sin, but a consequence of it, liberated and not created by it, even though it may lead, often enough, to actual sin. Man was not meant to endure this tumult, even during his period of growth, but it is co-natural in the growing, multiplex man, and could have been kept in harmonious peace only by preternatural help now lost to us, and never owed to us. An "evil instinct", as we call it, may be due to a thousand causes—unhealthy physique; wrong upbringing, preparing false associations of ideas and readiness to respond to destructive stimuli; to a bad environment itself the result of the long sinful history of man; or to the massive consequences of personal faults. Put it thus. A child who died "in original sin" alone, could not have the consequences of a supernatural life that it did not possess. But neither could it receive positive punishment for sins that it never had committed. Its destiny, then, would seem to be just what is suited to innocent human nature as such, and this appears to be a perfect natural happiness. Yet the very fact that it has this, and no more, imports a "deprivation": it is not what God would have wished it. When Catholic writers allude to the "wounds" inflicted by original sin upon nature, they either mean the total results of original sin that by now have issued into the darkening of our intelligence and weakening of our will, or the injury that nature as God foresaw and wished it, namely, supernaturalized, has received. This certainly is St. Paul's doctrine: no one now holds that he, or even St. Augustine, or the historical Church at large, taught the essential corruption of human nature such that every action of man is in itself bad and hateful to God—even his would-be good deeds. We earnestly beg that no reader will forget this substantial distinction between nature and super-nature, for without it, practically no single Catholic doctrine can be understood. It will be difficult to remember it, for, save by Catholics, this doctrine is to-day no more explained, we seem to see, to anybody.

Did God so withdraw His gift as to leave man without hope of regaining it? No, as the exquisite legend tells, He marked "even then" the tree that should be the ancestress of the Cross. But the Cross is not the first in the series of "salvational" dogmas. How did man lose his supernatural life? By incorporation with Adam, who lost it. "In Adam all died." How should he regain it? In many ways God might have restored it; but He willed that by incorporation with a Second Adam, a new Head to the human race, in whom that Life should be, man should be reinstated. "In Christ shall all be made alive."

How was this New Adam to be obtained? Many "ways" were open to God. But He acted, as St. Paul keeps saying, according to His super-abounding mercy, His over-brimming love, that "*not* as the sin was, the Grace should be". He sent to us one who was no mere "graced" man, but man indeed, yet source of grace, giving His gift because He had it, and having it because He was it, and being it not by prerogative but by nature. Hence that ecstatic paradox—"Happy fault of Adam!" that has earned for us so much more than it lost.[1]

The dogma then of the Incarnation is that the Second Person of the Holy Trinity took up a human nature, and, being born of the Virgin Mary, appeared among us, true God and true Man, One Person.[2]

So clearly was the true Divinity of Christ preached by the Apostles, that among the earliest Christians some could not see how this could be true, and also that His manhood could be a true one. Already St. John is seen resisting this nascent error that equipped Christ with a phantom body only. Reaction then tended to mitigate His divinity: He was not God, but "divine": this reached its climax in Arianism, and the heresy is having to-day its active vogue. The Church, however, defined the true Godhood of Christ, and the theory was forthwith hatched that these two true Natures must therefore be connected

---

[1] It would be out of place to linger upon the speculation that has captivated many minds—that whether or no Adam had fallen, the Incarnation yet would have taken place, so that sin or no sin, Christ would have been All in all. We return to this briefly below, p. 96.

[2] No Catholic of course supposes that the Divinity of Christ depends in any way on His virgin-birth or exacted it. That He was so born, is a separate dogma and cannot be denied. Its manifold appropriateness and utility is obvious; but it was freely chosen among the many ways in which our Redeemer might have come amongst us. We must add, in view of a constant and inexplicable confusion of language among non-Catholics, that "Immaculate Conception" does not mean virgin-birth, but is another dogma, namely, that Mary was raised to the supernatural level from the first moment of her human existence, by the infusion of grace, as we are in baptism.

by some artificial or moral link alone. The Church defined
that He was truly One Person. This unity of Person
made men think, then, that the two Natures in Him must
be somehow fused, and above all the mystery of His Will
began to trouble minds. After the due definitions had
been made, Christological heresies paused on the whole
(apart from sheer denials) till our own day, when, psychology also being invoked, a new theosophy would
express our Lord as but a man appropriated by, or over-
shadowed by, or even inhabited by the Divine, so that
the pendulum has swung back nearly all the way. Catholic
dogma persists in saying that He was, and is, True God,
True Man, One Person.

And on this dogma not only our theology depends,
but our devotion. Of what avail to men were a Christ
whose manhood were but spectral, who had not truly
this our flesh, nor truly a soul with all that the human
soul can endure—a human soul! When you have said
that, what have you *not* said? A soul, then, so united
with his body that indeed He is a human man and our
brother? And were He not God, how wrecked would
have been the very idea of that *unitive action* that pursues
itself throughout the Christian organism on the model of
that unsurpassable One-ing? Or, more simply, for which
of the Saints do we—who know well what Saints are—
feel what we do for Him who, were He not true God,
would be but a Saint after all? But this is not the place
to insist on what the heart can feel because of what the
intelligence is taught, about Christ. We have now to explain
the Work that He could do, and did, because He was what
He was.

4. OPUS CHRISTI

Man having refused to God that perfect homage which
God wished from him, and that he owed, was doubly

incapable of pleasing God. Deprived of Grace, he could not even begin to offer that supernatural love and worship that God wanted: and, deprived of many a preternatural help, he morally could not, and actually did not, pay even natural obedience to his Lord, but fell into innumerable sins, as he still does. But Christ, being true Man, offered in all things human actions to God, but, being God as well as man, in one Person, made all those human actions, divine actions. But the work of a divine action is infinite. So that what Jesus Christ did was indeed human, yet infinitely meritorious. Finally, if it be possible for any other man truly to incorporate himself with Christ, he gains the value of Him with whom he is incorporate, and his actions, more than intertwined with Christ's, truly "Christ-ed", have Christ's value before God. Such is the Christian mystery. If a man be incorporate with Christ, God, looking upon His Son, sees that man within Him; looking on the man, He sees Christ. When Christ praises God, I in Him am offering that praise: when Christ offers Himself to God, He offers me in Himself, I Him in myself, and myself in Him.

The moment this has been said, the mind travels in different directions over the field of Catholic doctrine, for so living is its tissue that, touch but one part of it, all of it vibrates. But naturally what we have said sends our thought to that Act done upon Mount Calvary, to which the consummation of our Redemption was divinely attached. It is clear that once we have the supernatural life circulating once more in our veins, we are re-instated in that Grace-world where God would have us be. It has also been said that not without incorporation in Jesus Christ can this be done. That such incorporation might be possible, our Lord not only had to become Man, but, as man and for man, to offer to God the perfect homage that we guiltily refused. Now any action of His was fit to achieve this, as we have also said. Yet not just any action of His was regarded by God as having redemptively achieved it. The Eternal Father attached the world's Redemption to the consummation of our Lord's life upon the Cross. Why? Put it thus, speaking ever humanwise. The Son of God, having resolved to take up our human nature, resolved to take it up wholly, and as we know it—that is, a human life in its entirety, including birth from a human mother; childhood; work; and even that most human experience of all, that death is. From not one natural event in the working out of His human life would He exempt Himself. The interplay of human wills in His regard should remain unchecked. Being by nature and in origin God, He would not think the being treated as God a thing to be held on to at all costs, but "emptied Himself" of all this; became, to the outward eye, merely man; and subordinated Himself yet further to death itself, and that, a death upon a cross (Phil. ii. 8). To take the easier, in itself legitimate, way was a true "temptation" to Him, and a recurrent one. But He had willed never to "favouritize" Himself; He worked no miracle on the stones that His Body might receive its much needed nourishment; He would make no flamboyant descent from the clouds, angel-upborne, into the Temple courts that He might forthwith be acclaimed Messiah. He might, in His agony, have asked for the Twelve Legions of Angels, but His own resolve had made this now impossible, even as on the Cross He would not "save" Himself. Therefore, while not one of His sufferings was "necessary", and while not one of them did He, as it were, deliberately engineer for Himself, yet all of them He freely and inclusively willed, and His Father, willing Him to save the world, and sending Him thereto, willed with Him all that Passion. Therefore it was on the Cross that He offered Himself to God as the perfect Sacrifice of praise, of thanksgiving, of expiation, of intercession, for the race, and on the Cross was accepted. Hence by the Cross and Passion of our Lord, by His precious Blood there shed and His death there died, we are redeemed. Christ there freely became That with which we can at last incorporate ourselves, and thus regain our due existence, that of Sons of our God.[1]

But Christ not only died upon the Cross but rose again, and the Church has ever taught the physical reality of His resurrection. Christ, having become man, will never cease to be so. And His Life conquers throughout Himself. His Body was no mere instrument, discarded contemptuously when it had enabled Him to die. With His Risen Self we are incorporate. And forthwith begins the continuous Opus Christi, the Energizing of Christ throughout the ages. And that work will be like Himself, twofold, for He is God and man, and suited to us, who also are twofold, body and spirit. His work will be at once spiritual and material; visible and invisible; eternal, yet inaugurated in time; heavenly, yet upon this earth; already begun, yet not completed. "Christ has not yet reached the full stature of His maturity." He is still fully fulfilling Himself, by means of us, till He becomes All, in all. Constantly men are implanting themselves in Him, building up His Body, making up in their own flesh what is lacking in that Body. So true is it that as without the Head the body would die, so without the Body the Head is meaningless. The perfect Christ is Jesus and His Christians; yet not His Christians numerically added to Himself, but He and they in one; in solidarity; we, "in" Christ; and we, alive, yet no more *we*, but Christ living in us.

---

[1] It would be out of place to discuss the various theories of sacrifice. Whatever they contain, the perfect sacrifice of Christ upon the Cross contains and transcends it.

Small wonder then that the structure of the Church herself is visible and invisible, material no less than spiritual. It is sheer Manicheanism to wish it otherwise. And we began by describing her sheer skeleton, so to call it, with that kind of brutality that is inseparable from all material things. But a skeleton is not the living man, nor a map, a country, still less the life lived within it. Yet the skeleton must be there. Without it, the man would collapse like a jelly and liquefy. We described, then, her Government. The Church is fully human, and full humanity involves Society; therefore the all-inclusive Res Catholica will be a society. No society is possible without government, as bond of cohesion, organization, origin of direction. Nor did Christ leave His Church without visible government. Not one item in it dare we tamper with. Apart from it is anarchy. Yet the government of a folk is not the life of the folk. We must try now to study the Church's life.

5. THE SACRAMENTS

It follows almost necessarily from the above that the whole Catholic concept of Christ's work is "sacramental". Since the Incarnation all religion should be incarnational. This double nature of our worship rises from the level of mere "significance", like what ritual or symbolism supplies to our senses and thence to our thought, through what we call "sacramentals", physical objects for one reason or another specially annexed to what much helps our soul, like holy water, blessed medals, and the like, up to Sacraments properly so-called. We hold that Christ Himself instituted in their substance seven transactions, so to call them, by means of which Grace is signified and also caused, provided we interpose no obstacle. Some time ago it became a fashion to use the word "magic" in connection with Catholic sacraments. Unmannerly folks, who appreciate not even what is meant by Magic, let alone Sacrament, still use it in popular prints. By "magic" is meant the coercion of divine (or even physical) activity by physical means known to a minority (as a rule) but discoverable by all. By lighting a fire, I make the sun shine. By uttering a secret Name that I know, I control a spirit. But if I use a Sacrament, I use what I know God to have freely appointed and authoritatively imposed on me: I use it freely and intelligently or else I gain nothing by my action; nay, if my will be not in a relation of obedience to God's will, I fail to gain what I want, Grace, its birth, its invigoration, or its restoration. And without revelation, I should not so much know that it existed, nor that I could get it, nor how. That in the supernatural order He had willed that I should address myself to the getting of grace partly by physical means who am part physical, is no stranger than that in the natural order I should have so been made by Him as to have to think dependently on a brain. But let me add two points. A Catholic dictum reminds us: *Non Deus obligatur sacramentis, sed nos.* It is not God who is tied by the Sacraments, but we. And *Facienti quod in se est, Deus non denegat gratiam.* To him who does what is in him, God does not refuse Grace. That is, if a man does not know about the Sacraments, or cannot get them, God can make it up to him in a thousand ways. And if a man honestly thinks he is using a sacrament—if for example he asks for Communion from one who is no priest but whom he thinks is—or if he really thinks there *are* no sacraments, but does what he can and would do more did he know how to, the mistaken worshipper will not go without his grace. Converts often fear that they will be asked to deny those gifts of grace they think, or "feel", they have received at the Holy Table. By no means. On the occasion of that honest and prayerful act, God gave them grace, more grace, doubtless, than the careless Catholic through his valid Communion. Not of course that the fact of the gift can be assessed by the feeling of the recipient. Such impressionism is as far from the Catholic doctrine as the magical mechanism alluded to above. But God's will towards man is good; if man's will, too, be good, well, that already is God's gift, and more will follow.

Christ then willed that we should enter alike into the visible Church and His invisible Body by means of Baptism. From our parents we are born, once for all, into our co-natural kingdom of the earth. By water and the Spirit we are born, anew and from above, into God's kingdom. From children of men, we become sons of God. As we cannot be born twice, so Baptism cannot be reiterated:[1] so vital is it that it be given, that the Church has always known that anyone, cleric or lay, male or female, heretic or pagan, can validly administer this sacrament provided he but use the true material, water, and the true formula, the Trinitarian one, and have the intention of *baptizing*. We add, the common sense of the doctrine of "intention" is clear from this: No sane person would suppose he had really baptized one to whom he should merely administer an exterior rite in order to show him "how it was done". If it be said that a baby at any rate cannot have the intention of *being* baptized, we hold that the Church intends its baptism; and that with the mystical unity of the Church, that of the family and the responsibility assumed by the sponsors (for no child may be baptized that is likely to live but not to be able to be brought up Catholic) are not out of keeping. Finally, one who cannot find a baptizer (you cannot baptize yourself!), but wishes to be baptized, is baptized "by desire", nor need this be an explicit desire for baptism, but a desire to do God's will, which would

---

[1] When a neophyte is received into the Church, baptism is administered outright if it is certain he never had been baptized: conditionally, if his baptism had occurred, but was doubtfully valid; not at all, if he had certainly been validly baptized.

include being baptized if he knew about it. And an unbaptized martyr has expressed the uttermost of that desire and is baptized in his own blood.

There is a physical adolescence, and a mental one, though by no means usually coincident with it. New powers are developed, new tendance is called for. In an analogous way a moment of spiritual adolescence occurs, when a child can take stock of its responsibilities. That the Sacrament of Confirmation is appropriate to this, all can see. Oil, with the laying on of the hand of (normally) a bishop, is the vehicle for this. Oil, in days of Hellenic athleticism and Hebrew tradition, stood for vigour, health, and consecration. And as adolescence happens only once, so Confirmation, like Baptism, impresses a "character" on the soul, a spiritual stamp that cannot be obliterated, nor can you be baptized, or confirmed, twice.

A crisis in human life occurs when a man wills so to join his human life with another as to create a truly joint life, that is, to *complete* his life by loving faithful union with one who similarly completes her life by union with his: and thus is laid the only sure foundation for that true human unit, the family. Far from scorning that contract between two, God establishes its permanence by making it the vehicle for grace, the material coefficient in a sacrament. Marriage becomes the very image of the wedlock between Christ and His Church. For even as He wedded His human nature to the divine, never to be separated, so He joined to Himself His Church, never to divorce her. In dim yet substantial likeness to that wedlock must Christian marriage be. Our Lord has reinforced the tendency of human nature by ordering that Christian marriage must be both monogamous and indissoluble; there is a level of likeness below which it must never sink. For a Catholic, then, by no mere disciplinary rule of the Church but by Christ's order, that echoes nature's hint, there is no such thing as divorce. The Church, regretfully, may sanction separation between two who cannot live happily together, but they remain married; there is no question of new marriage for either, till one be dead. And Church, like State, may fence wedlock with conditions, for the protection of the marriage contract, the disregard of which may cause a marriage to be null from the outset. Those incidents in history that are quoted as "Catholic divorces" were all of them nullity cases. Because the Pope could not allow, not a divorce, but a pronouncement of nullity, to the animal-minded Henry, he had to lose England's allegiance. Moreover, since we may not set moving natural processes only in order to defeat them, the Church will not hear of that artificial birth restriction which to-day is injuring the nerve-tissue of the nation, debauching its psychology, preparing its economic ruin, dissolving the ultimate bond of social cohesion, substituting convenience for principle, stifling the consciences of the married, and enabling young people at large to indulge their sexual instinct apparently without paying for it. To call this "disseminating knowledge" is but bluff. As well approve of the sly information of private schools or the coarse frankness of the streets (which is indeed far preferable). A few ill-examined facts, set in a false perspective, concerning health and population, and a few other facts, mechanical ones enabling a human to act like an animal without responsibility, do not provide knowledge. Spiritual self-control is the only method fit for application to humanity; mechanical self-coercion or frustration is as repulsive to civilized feeling as it is hostile to Christianity.

We may here add that the Church is only too well aware of the abominable social conditions said to necessitate the artificial restriction of births. The guilt of the distracted individual may well be indefinitely lessened by the ferocity of his temptation, and the guilt of those whose rapacity and self-worship accounts for the conditions and the temptation be increased. But she cannot compromise a principle. The Catholic doctrine of sexual morality is absolute. She requires chastity in each, according to his state. The unmarried must seek completely to control themselves in thought, word, and act; and this should *be* control, not repression merely. That is, they should not concentrate on a human instinct, to suppress it, but on a richer, still more human ideal, to achieve it. The married should be faithful to one another absolutely, that is, using the powers and rights that are theirs in subordination to the complete human and Christian ends. The doctrine of chastity is not based on any notion of the badness, or even corruptness, of the "flesh" and its instincts and functions; though owing in part to our enfeebled heredity, but far more to that torrent of sexual suggestion that the world at large administers to the average man, in which pseudo-science to-day plays as large a part as ever did the theatre or art, heroism is demanded of many to-day, in order to live well the *ordinary* Christian life. The Church has never been afraid of asking for heroism, and can help us thereto, and indeed it is the only worthy response to Christ who loved and served us beyond the dreams of heroism, whose mystical body we are, and whose limbs (as St. Paul with his terrible realism says, 1 Cor. vi. 15) we must not subject, in our own person, to the uttermost indignity. Since each Sacrament provides not only grace in general, but grace suited to the particular part of life with which the sacrament is concerned, marriage, therefore, helps the married in their special joys, trials, and vocation.

When a man is called by God to serve Him directly and actively and wholly, special help is certainly needed by him. The sacrament of Order, the plenitude of whose exercise resides in the episcopate, waits him. A priest's essential office is to absolve, as Christ's representative, and to offer and administer the Eucharist. Of these we speak below. His other functions, like teaching, shepherding, are real, but subordinate and in many ways shared. All good things may be misused, and each has its specially probable misuse annexed to it. Thus a priest, having sacrificed human home and its due affections, may grow hard. He may, having to teach authoritatively, extend his sphere of authority and be autocratic. He may be selfish. Against all such personal faults he will have to guard, as the financier and the landlord must guard against theirs. At least let it not be said that the priest stands between the soul and God. No more than the neck does between head and shoulders. If it be insisted that communication with God must be immediate and only so, we say it can be, and is, though not only so. That was not God's method, as we have said. He provided a human Christ. There is a written Bible. And our human thought veils God, whose vehicle it is. All existence may hold God and bring Him to us, and may hide God and steal Him from us. Only a bishop can ordain a priest, who cannot be unpriested. He must intend to be ordained, and the bishop to ordain him; and very briefly we add that we cannot possibly suppose that the ordaining bishops after the Elizabethan religious revolution wished to make, any more than the populace after a while wished to receive, the same *sort* of priest as before. Had you said to any of them, Do you propose to ordain or to become, do you desire to accept, a "massing-priest"? the answer would always have been No. The alterations in ritual and prayer-book have to be looked at in the light of this state of mind. A structural change in mind and will had taken place; with a ferocity such that we can but think it of Satanic origin, Mass became hated, and was to be eliminated. With the will to have Mass went the will to have, and to make, Mass-priests.

Little need be said of the "Last Anointing" which,

along with Viaticum, the Church's "journey money" in her tender parlance, constitutes the "Last Sacraments" needed by a man in that final crisis that bodily death is. None can rehearse it: all must endure it: everything hangs upon it. Then the will is fixed, and that fixing of the will fixes Eternity. When the body is failing and the brain is clouded, when thought hesitates and choice depends almost wholly (save for Grace) on habits formed of old, divine help is as never before necessary. When the consecrated Oil touches senses and limbs, avenues through which the soul has sought material for sin, the soul is strengthened, traces of sin are weakened or annulled; even to the body God often restores health, or at least, relief from distracting pain. Working up from the level of nerves, or even mind, and excluding due thought of God, a psychologist may find sufficient explanation in auto-suggestion of those wonderful experiences familiar to priests who administer this sacrament; but one who knows that God *is*, and somewhat of what He is, and of His Providence, and that Christ appointed this sacrament, has no temptation to rationalize its effects away.

But these are "crisis-sacraments". No man lives wholly by crisis, nor on oxygen alone. He needs his daily food and periodical doctoring. He can starve, poison, wound, even kill his body. Can he do anything like this to his supernatural life? Yes; by sin. Man can sap his spiritual life by seldom or never praying; can poison it by bad literature; by lesser faults can wound it; by "mortal" sin can slay it. For a sin to be mortal, I must know that God has forbidden it seriously: true, I can have an ill-informed conscience, and think He has gravely forbidden what He has not, like amusing myself on Sunday, or has not forbidden what He has, like spiritualism or divorce. But the point is, if I honestly think God has seriously forbidden such or such an act, and commit it, I sin; if I honestly do not think He has forbidden it, I am guiltless. This implies that not all wrong acts are equally grave, nor are they, though a trivially wrong act may take a grave colour from its circumstances. For circumstances and intentions specify acts. But we deny the Stoic or Calvinist doctrine that all acts that are wrong at all, are equally wrong.[1] It implies too that there can be an innocent ignorance as there can be a culpable one. To kill my parents and eat them is, really, murder and always wrong in itself: but if I honestly think that so to treat these aged and effete persons is a filial kindness, since I transfer their souls into my sturdy young body, and also, keep the family continuity intact, guilt is not imputed to me. To say "I did not know" is probably no help in a police-court. One is expected to know the law. But with God, who sees my conscience, the plea stands. Moreover, I must be sufficiently free to choose. If, tricked into gulping down a glass of gin that I thought water, I get drunk and break the street-lamps, I *could* not choose, and am morally guiltless, though it might be idle to tell a magistrate so. But God's judgment remains other.

Suppose that with adequate knowledge and choice I have gravely violated God's Law? My supernatural life is slain. Can it be restored? Yes. God gives a "second plank" to my soul in its drowning sin. Christ instituted the

---

[1] How does intention " specify " an act ? Some think that the formulas: " Do evil that good may come "; and, " The end justifies the means," are equivalent. No. The former is always false. You never may do evil with a " good " intention. The truth of the latter is obvious to anyone who understands what the words mean. It was but a chance that the formula did not grow up in the shape: The end vitiates the means. The subject under discussion is: Neutral acts—like asking a man to dinner. If my invitation be part of a plan to murder him, the evil end vitiates that neutral act. My invitation is part and parcel of my sin—willed by an evil will. If I ask him to dinner to keep him from bad company and help him towards good, my good purpose imparts goodness to—"justifies" i.e. "makes positively righteous"—my whole procedure. In a word: A good purpose or end justifies, a bad one vitiates, an act in itself neutral but ordered by me to the accomplishment of those several purposes. That is all that the formula means, has ever meant, or could mean.

Sacrament of Penance, wherein a sinner who knows of it must seek absolution. Absolution is not identical with Forgiveness. If I sin, and then execrate my act by "perfect contrition", with the intention of seeking absolution, forthwith my sin is forgiven. Contrition means being sorry for my sin with God somehow for my sorrow-motive. If I regret it just because it has cost me money, health, or reputation, that is remorse, not contrition. "Perfect contrition" does not mean that you could be no sorrier—who might not do yet better than he does?—but, that your motive is beyond bettering, namely, the Love of God. To have this motive is not hard: a man of decent feeling sees readily that he can be sorry for having offended God who has been so good to him, and is so good: mere fear seems to him somewhat sneakish. Such at least is my experience of ordinary men. But the moment he says: "My God, I am sorry", from this motive, intending to go to confession, his sin is forgiven: were he to die forthwith, he would be saved, for grace has been restored. We can, then, be sorry because God is so good, and so good to us; because Christ suffered and died for us; because heaven attends on virtue, hell on sin. Yet a mere "servile" fear of hell will not avail a man. Should he say: "I will not sin, else I should go to hell, but had God not thus threatened me, I certainly would and wish I could", he is not contrite. He is sinning in his heart, even though no outside act intensify, prolong, and diffuse his evil will. But along with this contrition must go "firm resolution" no more to offend God, grace helping him. If I say I repent, but I propose to sin again, or at least do not put my will on the side opposite to the sin, I have not repented. There may be here a double confusion in non-Catholic minds. A man says: "Alas, I don't feel sorry." Perhaps not. Being sorry and feeling sorry are two different things. I cannot simultaneously have the emotions proper to being in love, and those proper to being seasick. But a man does not cease to love his *fiancée* because he is seasick. Contrition is in the judgment and the will, and may or may not overflow into the feelings which are tricky things at best. We have seen the very hard-bitten, who have long since run through the emotions, profoundly contrite: the effervescently sorry soon may simmer down; the illusion of sorrow had been present. Or, a man says: "Never could *I* guarantee not to sin again. I know myself, my likings, habits, moods, and what becomes of my resolutions." But he is not asked to guarantee. Human nature is far too fluctuant to permit of guaranteeing anything. God asks him to resolve, and such as God sees his will to be, such is the resolution He expects from it. Moreover, Christianity is co-operative: the man contributes his poor 1 per cent of will-power, God gives the rest, and all of the Grace. Alone, he would certainly fail: with God, why should he?

All things can be misused: therefore the confessional. Yet its sheer utility is immense. Psychology keeps saying how wise it is to provide an outlet—to remove weights. Confession does so, though not for that was it instituted. Nor yet for the "spiritual direction" that may indeed be sought in the confessional, and that is so invaluable to adolescence. Yet this too is a by-product. Far from shifting responsibility on to the confessor, confession, it has well been said, makes the whole of life responsible. For each act now must be remembered (if possible), judged, and honestly valued. No Catholic may say: "Ah, I did so and so. But I don't want to remember it. I tried to forget it at once." Forget it, yes; but not "at once". Not till you have looked at yourself, judged yourself, and resolved about your future. This very process, moreover, strengthens the will and prepares that better future, especially if a man sees well that confession as such has nothing directly to do with character, but that that is for him to consolidate day by day. The taunts about "confessing to a mere man" are, I suppose, obsolete. No one imagines that Catholics feel that that is what they are doing, or that the confessional is a human institution. Nor in that most impersonal tribunal does the priest as a rule so much as know who is speaking to him: save for that Christ-like tenderness that he must show towards each soul, the less "personal" he is the better. If for the sake of sheer direction he has to know his penitent yet he must not ask more detail than necessary, nor certainly, save in the rarest cases, a name. What he does learn is, of course, covered wholly by the "secret" of the confessional which is absolute: save within the confessional, or with his penitent's express leave, no confessor can make any use whatsoever of what he has heard. Indeed, for most priests, I think, a kind of psychological barrier is interposed between his confessional, and his general, knowledge of a penitent. The two worlds are quite out of contact. A detail or two. The discipline of Confession has on the whole become more gentle, though all mortal sins must be confessed before Communion is approached: only the rarity, publicity, and severity of the earliest system have been modified as temperaments have changed. When death is imminent, a penitent says what he can: at that hour any priest, with or without permission to hear confessions, even excommunicate, has right to absolve all sins, even those "reserved", such is their gravity, to the highest authority. Finally, should an act of injustice be confessed, the penitent has to promise to put it right, if possible, before he can receive absolution. Before leaving this subject, we should like to insist that this discipline of Penance is, experience definitely shows, a simple, strengthening, and very sane affair; and lest a priest err through severity, he is wise often to recall not only the gentleness of Christ, but the great mystery of God's mercy, who is willing to preserve, even in a soul that has sinned and still is sinning, those two great supernatural graces of Faith and of Hope, whence all other virtues may proceed and which must necessarily precede them. And recall that no Sacrament is merely a *getting rid of wrong*. Sacraments give grace, a lead not only *from* but *to*. Hence the value of "Confessions of Devotion", when no grave sin is confessed, but more grace against sin is sought.

Man, we said, needs his daily food. In the Holy Eucharist this is given him, and in a way that suits the whole of him, body, mind, and supernatural life. The appropriate food of the body is meat and drink; that of the mind, ideas; that of the supernatural life must, in some sense at least, be Christ Himself, since that life is in a true sense His life. And Reality seems to me the best word to use about this Sacrament. All in it is really Christ, save those "appearances" that mercifully are left for our senses to recognize. We are not fed on memories, nor hopes merely, nor metaphors, nor what cannot be put simply to the simple. What simpler than the words, "This is really Christ: it is not bread"? We are in no way ashamed of saying we know not "*how* this thing shall be"; but that it *is*, the Church has always taught, and the word she has consecrated and embedded in her dogma, "transubstantiation", tells us but little more than that a change of reality has been effected, and that it is not what certain thinkers have said it is. What, after all, does the Church mean by "substance"? That which makes a thing to be what it is; what the thing really is. Less than ever nowadays ought we to want to say that a thing *is* colour, weight, whatnot that strikes the senses; more and more easily, we should have thought, can we emancipate ourselves from the idea that bulk, size, motion are the thing itself—of its substance. To speak quite strictly, Christ, present in the Eucharist, is present more like a spirit than "like" anything else: yet even that is not quite accurate. He is present there substantially and sacramentally. He does not rise when the Host is lifted, "nor move when carried in procession". But I should say that since He has willed that the appearances should survive, upborne by His reality, He is willing that we should allow ourselves devoutly to approach Him as in some sense, at least, localized. Nor do we think it is at all a good thing to treat the Eucharist over-philosophically. So inadequate is the appreciation that most men have of Reality, that philosophy might make a man go further towards feeling as if Christ were not really present, than it would instruct his mind about that Real Presence. Modernists used always to mock at the idea of our Lord's Ascension, as heaven is not "above" us. And we have heard our tabernacles derided as though it were a sort of baseness in religion to want any sort of localization at all. But men are not mere minds nor even mere philosophers. Nor did Christ dream of treating them as if they were. If He had, He never would have become Man. Is He Himself to be rebuked, for having "raised His eyes to heaven" at the first Consecration, as if heaven were "up", or raised His hands in blessing, as though the benedictions were a physical rain upon the heads of the apostles? And is Our Lady to be lessoned if she felt the house at Nazareth empty, when once her Son had left it on His Mission? Of course not. And we are right to feel our Churches desolate when, on the evening of Good Friday, Our Lord is no more sacramentally therein.

Christ, then, is not inside the bread, nor permeates the bread, nor can we easily conceive a mind so crass as that which suggested that Catholics believe in some sort of chemical change in the bread. Nor is the bread simply exchanged for Christ: but the term of the divine action which first was bread now is Christ. There has been a passage from one reality to another.[1]

---

[1] It is remarkable that the Aristotelian term "accident", which almost alternates in his philosophy with Substance, does not enter into Catholic

Christ, then, who has taken means to be really present amongst us, and not only within the soul of each, wills that we should make full use of Him. Two uses are of His direct ordinance, and we are bound to profit by them: other uses are left to our devotion and the permission of the Church. (To say that because Christ ordained two uses for His sacramental presence, He excluded all other possible ones, is like saying that because the Incarnation was ordained in order that Christ might save us on the Cross, it excluded His playing with little children or going to marriage feasts.) Thus the Church, her Faithful waking up with delight, generation by generation, to the rich possibilities of the Eucharistic presence, permits processions, reservation, Benediction, and so forth, but would now forbid the celebration of many Masses daily by the same priest, the carrying of the Blessed Sacrament into battle by a devout general, or into the House of Parliament by a pious politician. The rich Eucharistic life of the Church develops age by age, and I suppose the greatest modern instance of this is the recurrence of Eucharistic congresses.

But of the two uses ordained by Christ we need say little of Communion, save that it is indeed a participation in Christ Himself and in His sacrificial work. Though the words of consecration by force of the spoken word place, as they say, Christ's Body under the appearances of bread, His Blood under those of wine, yet, because He can now no more die, Christ is wholly, where He is at all. Neither body nor soul nor blood nor divinity can ever be separated more. Hence not only the practice of the early Church, which gave

---

definitions, but they use "species", or appearances. So far is the believer in transubstantiation from being committed to a wholesale Aristotelianism. Aristotle's category of substance was found so useful to the Church, that she in fact made use of it, nor has anything better been elaborated, nor is it likely to be. This does not exclude the possibility of the doctrine of the Eucharist being stated, though probably less perfectly than in the official way, in other terminology, e.g. dynamic.

communion in several different ways, nor considerations of practical sorts, or of reverence, but theological considerations make it fully legitimate for the Church to ordain the administration of Communion under one Kind only, though she could alter this disciplinary law at any moment. Still, so grave are the objections attendant on the administration of the chalice, especially in the East, not to insist on foreign missions, nor the irreverences that we ourselves have witnessed in regard of it, that it is unlikely she will create a new rite that shall include the chalice. Canon Law, of course, explains itself at the outset as concerning the Latin part of the Church, and Rome does not alter Oriental rites save when true necessity, and reasoned request, force or beg her to. The social implications of Holy Communion cannot but be obvious.

In our paragraphs upon the second great use to which Christ wills the Eucharist to be put, the offering of our Lord in Mass, we wish to discuss none of the theories of sacrifice which can preoccupy theologians. Enough to say what we alluded to above, that Sacrifice at least includes an external offering to God as the source of all our being, and such therefore as cannot be offered to any other. In history, an element of destruction has very often entered into this offering, not because God needs or enjoys any such thing, but partly because the totality, irrevocability, and unicity of the offering are thus brought home to ourselves; and, because there is a true appropriateness in such an element being included, since sacrifice, in our guilty world, cannot but be sacrifice offered by sinners and because of sin, and there is an analogy between sin and destruction deserved and caused. Yet since sacrifice could have been offered in a sinless world, destruction on such an account does not enter into its essence. He who is the maximum of Being can take no pleasure in a thing being made less than it is or ought to be. However, since Mass is the commemoration of the Passion, it would seem that it could not adequately picture it forth, still less *be* it in the sense that we shall say, without such an element being in some way involved. For the Passion was essentially an offering for sinners and because of sin. Moreover, as we said, the salvation of the world was attached to the death of Christ upon the Cross. Enough then to say that the sacrifice of the Mass is simply the immortal sacrifice of Christ, though in Mass His Blood flows no more, nor is the sacrifice re-offered as though Calvary were insufficient, but in Mass each individual soul appropriates that Sacrifice and its fruits are applied to that soul.

Amazing to reflect that this is the one and only act, being accomplished every hour, nay, minute of every day, somewhere round our globe, because, and only because, nearly 2,000 years ago men were bidden: "Do this". The world holds nothing to compare with it.

We would ask, then, that what we said on p. 68 should be recalled. True, even though a man who assists at Mass be not "in grace", nor substantially united with Christ, yet he derives profit therefrom, inasmuch as the circumambient grace, so to call it, the very atmosphere of grace and the impetratory value of Mass, prepare his soul for contrition and intercede for him: and he can truly offer Christ, though not Christ-in-him, nor himself in Christ. But when a man is "in Christ", forthwith he and Christ are vitally united, and Christ offers Himself and His Christian in Himself, and the man offers Christ and himself in vital unity, and God, looking upon Mass, sees both His Son and those who are "in one" with Him. Hence you cannot but perceive the incredible cogency of Mass. It is a gift that God cannot resist: the priest, and the layman too, since there is a solidarity between them, and the priest is but the instrumental cause of the offering of Mass, have omnipotence in their hands. Mass is an act—not a prayer recited, not a ceremony contemplated, but the supreme act of history, unequalled in the world. No wonder that the Church orders periodical assistance at Mass; no wonder such an act "sanctifies" a Sunday; no wonder that a man might feel that had he offered but one Mass in his lifetime, he would have justified his very existence. Nor is there any wonder that an historian sees that Mass is, as it always has been, the vital fact in the world of to-day, and in a mystical sense concentrates in itself Bethlehem, Calvary, and the Resurrection. It is Christ offering Himself to God, and God for ever accepting Christ.

6. THE SOUL'S DESTINY

We early said that the soul is indestructible. What then becomes of it when the body falls to pieces—dies, in short? The surviving soul is either in possession of the supernatural life, or it is not. If it is not, it clearly cannot perform the vital functions of a life it has not got. But (we speak here of the baptized Christian) a soul only has *not* got that life, because it has lost it, and lost it by its fault, and we are taught that at physical death the will is fixed—it has, as we said, exhaled itself into this or that kind of act, an act good or bad. If then a man as we say "dies in mortal sin", he has adequately expressed and for ever fixed himself in the hate of God. Such a soul is then said to be in "hell". Hell means the unalterable alienation from God. Once and for all, let us state clearly that all we are taught is, that *if* a man so dies in mortal sin, that is his doom. The Church tells us nothing about averages, or numbers of any kind. No man can assert of any one soul that it is lost.

Hell may be described in many ways, provided that we recollect that all of them appeal to the imagination and are no part of dogma. Even that "fire" of hell concerning which every Christian century has spoken, is definitely not that "fire of coal" which never could touch a spirit. It does not follow that this is a mere allegory. No Catholic could safely say that hell's "fire" is metaphorical only. It is, however, enough to say that the soul's punishment reaches it not only from within itself, but from outside things. And, indeed, how could it be otherwise? We need not linger over considerations such as the remorse that a lost soul feels, though that is real; but, recall the essence of the fact, that the soul which was meant to be united with God supernaturally, is disunited from Him, and thus, from all else that is united with Him. From all that is good, it is disunited, and all that is good becomes its source of anguish. For ourselves, were we to wish to talk of hell, we should use the word "loneliness". That which was meant for an incredible union is in the utmost isolation. That which in some sense was meant to be in organic vital communion with every manner of existence, has shrunk, through its chosen selfishness, into a point—a conscious point, to use a violent paradox. Even without revelation, it would be hard not to see that this is possible. Revelation *tells* us that it is possible, and how it can be achieved, and still more how it can be avoided. But it is part of the mercy of God that we should know that there *can* be "enduring consequences" of disaster, should we choose deliberately and gravely to offend Him, and to persevere in so doing. Actions do *not*, as they say, amount to "all the same" in a hundred years: life does not come out in the wash: we can corrupt the very texture of our self. Nor can we dream of speaking of "injustice", cruelty, in God; nor as though He created men to be damned: nor as though, if He saw a soul seeking to damn itself, He ought to coerce its free will into good. Were it for any reason whatsoever unjust that a soul should be damned, damned it would not be: each soul damns itself, "hells" itself: God has but to register the reality of what the soul now is—He sees it; He will not violently un-real-ize it, and so He "pronounces judgment". The word after all for "judgment" is in Greek that elusive word "krisis", and even in St. John you well can see how it hovers between the meaning Judgment and Separation. Enough. If the soul separates itself from God, if it tears itself out of the Body of Christ, it is not, and henceforward cannot be, united with God, living by Christ's life. God ratifies that.

If this tragedy has not happened, the soul has in it the supernatural life, and can enjoy its consequences. But its natural and supernatural lives may not yet be in perfect harmony. It may not be living all through itself with the Life of Christ. Indeed, if of no one we have known would we dare say that there is no good in him, of whom are we likely to surmise that they have reached an absolute perfection ? Keep to ourselves. We know well that were we to die to-day, there would still be much in us that was unlike God, antipathetic to God. Assuming, then, that grace was in me, I should be substantially united with God, yet not perfectly so. The Church teaches that such a soul passes into Purgatory, and of Purgatory she teaches little else save that our prayers can help souls that are there. Purgatory, as the name implies, involves purification, and Catholics have always spoken of that process as pain. Perhaps once more a crude analogy may help the imagination. Say that a rake falls in love with a girl in every way most perfect. Something has happened that makes him see her worth, and everything else in consequence, himself included, in a new perspective. The sight of his old life is anguish to him: yet that very anguish is a purifying one and full of joy, because he knows he could not go back to it: and this happy pain is making him more and more like the soul whose purity had thus revolutionized his scale of values and of judgments. In Purgatory we see our sins aright; that in itself is pain; and we joyfully accept what other punishment God may see fit to inflict, in His just mercy, upon us; all in us retires more and more from the very possibility of evil will, just because it is growing more like God, and it grows like Him, because sin is being positively wrung out of it. It is the opposite of hell; there the will hates God, and loves that sin which is its torment. Indeed, as our purgatory draws to its close, so pure will our love have become, that we shall wish our pain to cease, not because it is *pain*, but because it means that *God* is not yet able to be perfectly pleased with us.

We are told that owing to our organic union with Christ, with whom the souls in Purgatory too are united, we can actually assist them by our prayers, and indeed, how should we not, since even on earth we can help our fellow-men by praying for them? What more perfect consolation for the mourner, than to know that he need not merely "remember" his lost, but can help them? Indeed, "lost" is not the word he will like to use of those who are so much deeper in reality than he has reached. Many an one may even rejoice, when he reflects on the double chasm, this side and that, that separates on earth two personalities, that at least half the gulf is bridged, now that one of the two is united (as we can at least hope he is) with the Vision of all truth—God. If I do not yet adequately know him, he at least on his side may have advanced into a whole new world of knowing me. Add, that Catholics are forced to speak of the "next world" in terms of time. But it is a duration that has nothing to do, need we say, with the time that is measured by the motions of our solar system! Think, if you prefer, of Purgatory in terms of depth, of intensity. We cannot tell in what "dimension" a disembodied soul exists.[1]

[1] Spiritualism is forbidden to a Catholic. A spiritualist seeks to communicate with souls either to find out whether a next world exists—to do this would already be apostasy in a Catholic, who knows perfectly well that it does, because he is taught so: or, to get consolation by communi-

But suppose that a soul passes into the next world (as any soul leaves its Purgatory) perfectly united throughout itself with God. It is then "in heaven". It possesses the Beatific Vision, sees God as He is, and is inseparably united with Him. We do not see that we need, or even can, linger upon this. We must, however, add that the Church teaches the "resurrection of the flesh". By this is meant that we men for ever shall be men. Apart from its body, a soul is in some sort of violent state. But we have not to conceive our destined self as like what we now are: St. Paul uses a violent paradox and speaks of a spiritual body. Still, even to speak of it would have been waste of time, had he meant nothing more than "spirit", which the soul is in any case and cannot be more so, or twice over. Therefore we shall not in our immortality, "be naked minds", but men made perfect, as men united with God and all wherewith man may be united. Hence the artist need not fear

---

cating with dead friends. Catholics have other consolations; and anyhow, the spiritualist is cheated. For by no conceivable test could you tell whether this is indeed the soul of so and so with whom you are speaking. The only test offered is, if your medium mentions some incident that only you and the person who has died were aware of; for example, an act done in some else lonely place and never mentioned to anyone. But this would be useless; for such communications imply a belief that spirits exist. So, though no other living man saw that action, innumerable spirits may have been aware of it, and by any one of these the communication could be made. Nor can the medium's voice, for example, strangely like that of the dead man, provide any argument. For a voice is air thrust through a vibrating throat and so forth, and in no case is the medium's throat or tongue that of the dead person, so in no case will there be anything but an imitation, and who knows how many spirits might not be capable of that? Our personal reaction towards Spiritualism includes a conviction that quite seventy-five per cent of it is fraud; nearly all the rest abnormal but quite natural phenomena of a psychical or physico-psychical sort; and a small residuum may be due to the intervention of spirits which even without appealing to our Faith we should suppose to be of a degraded if not imbecile kind, assuming you can have an imbecile spirit. The effects on the nervous system have, so far as we have observed them, been uniformly bad; the ethical results, as on honesty, self-control, have been no less disastrous; and the intellectual level of anything we have ever read, from a spiritualist source (we mean terrestrial sources), has been incredibly low, and argued that the whole occupation was a sort of mental debauchery.

that only on this earth can he rejoice in colour or in form, nor here only is it that the musician will love sound. But all these joys and loves are at present, as we very well experience, more than half pain, and the minimum of union with the beloved, which is all we now achieve, keeps thrusting in upon us the anguish of our otherness. Perhaps we say enough when we repeat that to the human soul is open a destiny of ineffable union with Truth and Love and Beauty in itself, and wherever and however they exist, and, correspondingly, the possibility of separation from all these things.[1]

[1] We add a few lines on Indulgences. The Church has no control over the next world. But in this she has delegated authority from her Lord save, of course, in what touches the substance of that which He bequeathed to her. Every sin incurs a debt of punishment, and my punishment is not merely that alteration for the worse in myself that any sin involves, but, since I live my exterior and social life as well as my secret individual one, for this if for no other reason it is seen that temporal social punishment is quite appropriate. A father may forgive his son, but still insist that he endure due castigation. Many a lad would feel that he so deserved it, that he would even prefer to undergo it. The Church very early annexed certain punishments to certain sins, and these were called Canonical Penances, as, for example, fasting seven days for striking your father. As times grew softer, and temperaments more irritable, or the general moral level lower, she began to commute the punishment she herself had inflicted, and might substitute the recitation of seven psalms for those seven days of fasting. It is true that this was not strictly yet an "indulgence", but a commutation: there was still supposed to be some kind of proportion between the new penalty and the old one, and between the old one and the sin. But a real principle was laid bare when the Church made it clear that she remitted punishments in view of the overwhelming merits of the martyrs who died for Christ. Here was an appeal to the solidarity of Christians, and to the value of the life of each, for all, since that life was Christ's. In the long run, then, it became clear that the Church had the right to remit, quite simply, by the power of the Keys, the debt of temporal punishment that a man might owe, appealing to that vast treasure-house of merit that is ever being refilled by the labours of the Saints in Christ, and for Him. We have no call here to explain the abuses to which indulgences have lain open, though they no longer do so. Popular confusions may sometimes have arisen owing to theological language not yet adequately formed; but I hold it demonstrated that never at any time was an indulgence supposed to mean permission to commit sin; nor yet, " so many days off purgatory"; nor were indulgences as such ever sold (I allow, of course, for the sin of this or that individual; everything is bound to happen once or twice in the world's history; but I mean on any scale worth mentioning, or with official approbation). It was always understood that an indulgence

Finally, we have used the word "merit". It is an unpopular one. People say: "Let me do good because it is good, not because I want to earn heaven or escape hell." Others say: "All my righteousness is filthy rags. One, and One only, merits—Christ." As for the last statement, it is perfectly silly to talk as if a good act were not good. It may not be supernaturally meritorious, but it is good and cannot but have its suitable reward. On the other hand, it is manifestly true to say that no human act apart from Christ's salvific act, can merit anything supernatural whatsoever. This we have said all along. We have insisted that the Natural never can earn or merit, let alone develop into, the Supernatural, and the Church's critics, who, having struck her on one cheek, always go on with or without her permission to strike her on the other, are often found objecting to this very thing—that the Supernatural should be called wholly outside the merely human scope. But, once we are united with Christ, once we *are* Christ's Body, our actions, done "in Him", acquire the value of His: "in Him" we merit and are bound to. But it is the whole idea of working for reward that certain lofty souls dislike. No doubt it is good not to concentrate on what we hope to get or fear to lose. Serve God for the pure love of Himself, by all means. You are at once a Saint. But what, after all, is the fruit of our merit? What is it that we earn? God Himself. The fruit of any good action, once more, is that we *are* better. None can be indifferent to that. And supernaturally, what is the heaven that we earn? God, once more, and union with Him. The very thing we profess so much to love. We cannot *but* want it. We must needs

---

concerns *forgiven* sin; and even Tetzel's theology (since his name is always mentioned in this connection) was never at fault, so far as we can see. Finally, when an indulgence is said to be "applicable to the souls in Purgatory", this means "by way of prayer", that is, that we devoutly hope that God, on the occasion of our doing something that would win for us an indulgence, accelerates the purification of souls, or a soul, in Purgatory.

hope for it. The more we work for the love of God (which is already an effect of God's love for us and our increasing response to it), the more God loves us, and the more He rewards us by the communication of Himself. And as for fearing to lose that, how should we not? And even if we work partly just because we do not want to suffer, and do want to be happy, well, that is exactly what God wants for me Himself; and I am not going to be so superior as to tell God I don't want His offers, and am indifferent to His companionship in eternity.

7. THE SAINTS

We have also mentioned Saints. Saints are those whose souls are perfectly united with God. Who knows how many souls are thus purified while physical death has not yet been endured? Some few are "placarded" by the process of canonization; but the placarding of a Saint does not mean that no one else is a Saint. At any rate, in heaven all souls are Saints. We are allowed to pray to those who are there, for, I repeat, one blood flows in our spiritual veins. We are more than brothers: we are all Christ's Body. Nor, I think, does anyone who knows the working of the Catholic mind from within, imagine that the Saints oust God or our Lord from their unique pedestals. One's whole "address" to a Saint is totally different from our approach to God. You cannot even strike a proportion, and say: "Too much honour is given to Saints, in comparison with what is offered to Jesus Christ." Between two different sorts of homage no proportion can be struck. Two Catholic facts would suffice, after all, to preserve the Catholic mind in shape—one is the existence of Crucifixes, and the other, Holy Communion. Imagination and thought and will are bound to be kept as they should be, by these very simple things.

Catholics render, as all know, a unique homage to the Blessed Virgin Mary, mother of our Lord. In a book like this one may experience even a sort of shyness when speaking of the sacrednesses of our domestic intercourse, so to call it, within the divine Family that is ours. Enough to say, first, that we could think of no surer way of insulting so perfect a Son, than by neglecting or dishonouring His Mother. Do what we will, our homage for her must be unique, because she is so herself. No other woman in the world was chosen to be Mother of the Word made Flesh. And if we should expect any good son to do all he could for his mother, and so soon as he could, in the case of Jesus and Mary we are not disappointed. There was no alternative of benedictions needed—Mary had both blessings, being His Mother, *and* hearing God's word and ever keeping it. Not only are we right in naming Mary " Mother of God", since this title flows necessarily from what we have said of the divine personality of her son—she was mother of a Man who was God, not (in some strange way) mother of a *nature* merely, but God prepared her for that office foreseen by Him in His eternity. We are taught that to Mary from the first instant of her personal life was given supernatural grace. That is the Immaculate Conception. And this grace was ever preserved and augmented in her; she was never disloyal to her Son, but ever the "handmaid of the Lord", to whom her Saviour did indeed "great things", so that our generation, as all generations, gratefully calls her "blessed". Catholic devotion to Mary is the simplest thing in the world, and who shall ever assess the sheer value to the world of this figure of perfect womanhood that God in His goodness has placed within it?

We add here a consideration that is not part of Catholic dogma, and perhaps will never be, but which is dear to us, and seems to correspond with much that other dogmas

lead us to expect. We have spoken much of Christ as the
Head of the human race, summing up all things into
Himself. Recall that God's vision of that human race was,
in itself, and antecedently to Adam's sin (to use human
language that places "before" and "after" in the Eternal),
that of a graced and supernaturalized race. There is much
that makes us think that God had always meant to effect
the union that this implies, through His Son made man.
Not only, had this not been so, would one unsurpassable
form of union have been omitted in the marvellous history
of the Unification, Harmonization, of all things, but a
whole series of manifestations of God's love would never
have been actualized. Much that St. Paul says seems to
show not only the Second Person of the Blessed Trinity as
the complete explanation of the world, that came into being
through Him, is made intelligible by Him, and sets towards
Him—"*all* creation" travails and groans towards the
hour when the "sons of God" that we, through Christ,
are, shall be revealed—but the Apostle seems in all these
passages to visualize the Son of God as *Christ*, that is as
the Word made Flesh, and that, not only in order to redeem
us, now that we have sinned, upon the Cross, but that He
might indeed be God's "recapitulation" of creation—all
things, down to the humblest of God's creatures, find their
true meaning and existence in Christ. We are not merely
saved "*from*", but saved "*to*". If then, indeed, along
with the making of man, God willed that His Son should
Himself be made man, and (as we see) be born of human
mother, the most blessed Virgin Mary was always seen
along with her Son; always she has been the predestined
channel of God's favours to us; from eternity she has been
associated with the Word made Flesh; and the completest
expression of God's Will towards man is Mary with her
Child in her arms. Be this as it may, and it is a consideration on which our minds rest lovingly and with perfect

satisfaction, in the actual scheme of things Christ was given to our world through Mary, nor will we ever dissociate her name from His.

8. BEHAVIOUR

We hardly think that Catholic Ethic need here be described. After all, what Christianity has introduced is rather motive and ideal, than material or strict law of ethic. That is, the material of ethic is what it ever was, and can be seen in the Decalogue. But we are now bidden be "perfect" as our Father is perfect; and we must aspire rather than shun, and a perfect love must so far as possible cast fear out. Christianity has always altered life from within, rather than by coercion; it was not Law that changed the lot of the slave, the weak, and of woman. It was the new realization that men are brothers; and it is noticeable that this, which sheer reason might have taught us, was not as a matter of fact grasped in all its consequences till our brotherhood was seen to exist supernaturally in Christ. Difficult even now is the Church's task. Men do not like to draw the necessary consequences of their principles, and Catholics, as the world is realizing by now, have principles that involve consequences in every imaginable part of life. You have already seen that the Catholic doctrine about marriage affects the question of divorce, and how no part of life, married or unmarried, is not covered by the law of due chastity. The practical problem of birth-restriction too falls under the Catholic law, and most certainly that of the education of children. Catholics, it will be seen, ought to be good citizens; but there are regions within which the State is not paramount, nor may the State prevent a Catholic from bringing up his child a Catholic, nor should it make it difficult for him so to do, and it ought to facilitate his so doing. It should assist him to build and maintain those wholly Catholic schools within which a Catholic atmosphere reigns—Plato himself, had he possessed the word, would have declared that atmosphere is in its way as important for a child as sheer instruction is. Nor can instruction be properly given save by one who is convinced of the instruction that he gives; hence it may be taken as certain that Catholics will bleed themselves white rather than defraud their children, or allow them to be robbed, of their rights in this matter, especially the poorest and most helpless, on whom legislation is apt to bear most heavily. But while we hold to what we have just said about the poor, and those who have fewest "opportunities", as we say, we must not for a moment be taken as suggesting that the rich need less help. In one sense they need a deal more, since they are plunged in the complex illusion of wealth itself and position. They imagine so easily that those good things are good enough. Money means *power*, and nothing else breeds self-sufficiency so fast or is so likely to corrupt a man's perspective. And the backs of their minds easily get starved, both of principle and motive. Universities are good: but the education there received, should it amount almost wholly, as it often does, to mere instruction, coupled with criticism and analysis without construction, would be bad and dissipating, and this too it often is. Somehow Catholic education should last a whole life through. Nor will we for a moment admit that there *is* more "character" in the leisured or privileged classes. Those who preach reincarnation, have often the audacity to say (we have heard them) that dwellers in slums need reincarnation to give them the chances they have not had in "this" life, and which, they implied, they would need to make them able to become what We are. We have before now had to insist to an audience of pearled and feathered ladies, and to roomfuls of delicate-minded undergraduates, that we would be prepared to find more solid virtues, nay, more heroism if not sanctity, in barrack-room, stables, docks, mines, garages and the like, than in drawing-rooms and studies.

Not that we have any right to tolerate the outrageous social conditions in which men are now forced to live. Save in the sense that all men are God's sons and Christ's brothers, and hence our brothers too, they are in no sense "equal". There is not the slightest reason for suggesting that every man should have exactly the same measure of material comfort or even material education, so to call it, as every other. But every man has the irreducible right of living a proper human life, which does not mean just non-starvation. This has far-reaching consequences in all that concerns trade and business and finance, nor can I say that I can justly possess an indefinite amount of property nor do just as I please with it when I do possess it. That possession, or that use of what is possessed, which injures my neighbour, is a bad one. But, having said that the Catholic principle of justice and the Catholic ideal of charity have ramifying consequences of a very probing sort, I need go no further. Nor need I dwell upon the national and international consequences of the same law and ideal. The triumph of my nation in all circumstances cannot enter into a Catholic scheme. The question of war can be very accurately discussed by a Catholic; the question of revolution, of Communism and international finance or international strikes, or national, for that matter, or any strike or lock-out. The world has now been devastated by another and a far worse war, on the horrors of which we will not dwell, but we must emphasise the fact that generations of increasing scepticism have weakened or eliminated in whole populations the idea of *God*, so that eminent authorities even in our land have said that they know nothing of any "Law of Nature", but that Parliament is the sole source of law and therefore must decide what is right, what wrong. It ought to have become obvious after the 1914–18 war that

Law forbids them to be tampered with. Western Catholics are most familiar, naturally, with the Latin rite. The average man presumably regards it as the proper way of behaving in church and notices it but little. He may, however, most laudably develop a sense, and an appreciation of, the Liturgy. The Liturgy, simple and natural as were its beginnings, is, by now, an inexhaustible mine of spiritual beauty and riches. Mean indeed would be the mind that was not thrilled by the enthusiastic singing, by thousands of East End dockers, of the *Credo*, to plain chant, in Latin: or the singing by rough lads in a colliery town, or by Zulus of the psalm *Laudate Dominum omnes Gentes*, to another Gregorian rhythm, in the Latin tongue. The explanation of the Liturgy, in every detail, is a good, but not a necessary thing. Rather, as the Catholic feels that to abstain from meat on Friday is an irksome, yet the proper thing to do, and that those who do not, do not quite know how to behave, or, at least, that in their circumstances these points of ancient etiquette cannot be demanded of them; so he will expect that the dignified regulations of the Divine Court on earth shall be obeyed, but he will never be fussy about them, save in the sense that a member of the Heralds' College might be distressed by a violation of some venerable detail. In the abbreviated worship of "Low Mass", the ancient sober ceremony pursues itself to the satisfaction of the worshipper, who assists at the intimate reception of his King: in High Mass, still so sober and austerely Roman a transaction, more state is displayed: the Liturgy reaches its sublimest level in the ceremonies of Holy Week, of Consecration of Churches and of Bishops, and in papal functions, when the sublimity of the Office and the humility of its occupant are equally made manifest.

noble, vague ideals, based on humanity alone, had no chance at all against the determination of unscrupulous men and the selfish greed of individuals or groups. Making every allowance for the exhaustion of nerve and the shock to brains due to the second world-war, and the length of time that it takes for passions to grow quiet and suspicion to be disarmed, we have seen fear and vengefulness, lying and hate go on playing their destructive rôle and increasingly doing so; every doubt as to men's sincerity that we entertained during the war itself has proved justified and we have seen the frightful spectacle of one country, at least, condemning men for crimes of which itself was at that very time continuing to be guilty. So certain is it that Ethics, as such, have no chance of survival if they be divorced from dogma, nor can dogma, however much it may transcend reason, ever do without it.

It does not follow that every problem that is possible in the world has been thought out by Catholics: some have not yet been set; others are set, but the issue is still undefined: and still less does it follow that the application of Catholic principles is easy in the circumstances, which grow yearly more complex, so that the material to be judged very seldom lies clearly before the view. But it remains certain that the Catholic Faith is not concerned with other-worldly speculation alone: still less is it a quaint way of behaving inside a church: it is a universal philosophy that fears no part of life as material for its energizing: indeed, it demands that it should be applied to every part of life, from hygiene to art, from drink to mysticism. Else it would not be Catholic.

It may perhaps be not quite out of place if we insist that there is such a thing as Catholic asceticism and mysticism. All are called to a true asceticism, in so far as they are told to control themselves for reasons such as we have described, and that neither in body nor in mind are they their own master, and that not even art, which claims so often a curious sort of emancipation, has the right to it. Nothing in the world is quite autonomous. But everybody knows that the Saints, or many of them, have gone far beyond mere self-control, and have done severe penances. There are here two main principles: one is, that matter is not bad; the other is that, owing to our solidarity in Christ, we are able, still "in Christ", to offer our prayers, sufferings, and penances for one another. Paul fills up in his own flesh what still is lacking in the Body of Christ. It may be said that the history of Jesus accurately reproduces itself in the Church at large, though not equally in each individual. It will for ever be useless to try to uproot the Cross from any part of Christianity. Hence no cult of hygiene or comfort or wealth or of anything material has, a Catholic holds, any chance of success as an adequate end for Progress. You cannot so much as know whether you are progressing, if you do not know starting-point and goal and route. Physical well-being is no goal, and is scorned even humanwise by the noblest of mankind, and comfort is never the way to anything. Or, shall we say, Comfortableness. For Christ did promise us Comfort, but that He would make us comfortable, never.

"Mysticism" is a word used in so many ways that we shall write very briefly of what we mean by it here. In a sense, all Catholic doctrine, *as* revealed, is "mystical", since its source is not in ourselves: the whole supernatural life can also be called "mystical", since it essentially transcends human nature. But there have always been men (also in "paganism" and of course in heterodox forms of Christianity) who have sought a closer union with God than that which depends on the imagination (which cannot really represent Him at all) or on reason (which represents Him only analogically (see p. 9). This has often led them astray into disastrous illusions. It is, however, true that

chosen men and women have been called to a more direct vision of God and a more conscious union with Him than what reasoning on Him can supply: we have not to wait for the 11th or 13th or 16th century to know this as a fact, though documents become more plentiful then. We will, however, recall that the "mystical" life implies the ascetic one—the constant endeavour to root out, with God's help, all sin and attachment to sin from the soul: indeed the more perfect the union with God, the more probing will be His action, which denudes the soul of every trace of selfishness, and this denudation as a rule implies a period of complete spiritual darkness (St. John of the Cross's "Dark Night") in which the soul undergoes a true purgatory and loves God without return upon self—without what the Saints call any "property" in anything, even in self—without what St. Bernard calls the *curva voluntas*, the will curving back selfward instead of moving straight towards God and adhering to Him wholly. Nearly all non-Catholic "mysticism" disregards this purifying process; or again attaches importance to ecstasies and the like, which may indeed be intermediate marks of God's favour and of progress but in no sense constitute holiness, and even from these gifts of God (for they *are* not God) the soul must be detached; or again regard the active life as incompatible with the truly mystical life, which St. Teresa's career suffices to disprove; or actually regards the flesh as somehow evil and in consequence cannot admit anything incarnational and must turn its back on Jesus Christ— a caricature of mysticism to which alone, so far, Mr. Aldous Huxley's heroic attempt to understand the matter has attained.

A word on ritual. Catholics belong to different "rites" —the Slavonic, the Chaldæan, the Latin, the Coptic. Each is, as a matter of fact, the product and congenial expression of an entire and very ancient culture. Canon

PART III

THE CHURCH IN HISTORY

THE Catholic, then, contemplates the Church as founded by its wise and tender Lord with all His delicacy of touch and "unhurrying haste" and peaceful power. Scorning not even the simplest of His children, He chose no supermen for its first members and destined apostles: gradually He initiated them into the doctrines they were to teach in His name, and then sent them forth invested with grace they never merited to a work that no strength of their own could do.

Little by little, the organization of the infant Church reveals itself: accidental qualities and even, if you will, a childish charm disappear; essential articulations of structure, substantial functions, are defined. Absorbed at the outset almost wholly in affirming its freedom and then its very existence in face of the Jews, soon enough, owing to the Diaspora and then to the world-wide outlook and terrific energy and special mission and sublime revelation of St. Paul, it had to confront the Empire. Once more Christ stood face to face with Cæsar, and the Christians had to elect whether to worship the State instead of Conscience, and they suffered ostracism and then death itself sooner than succumb. The duel will be a lasting one.

Next, as men became converted who had been educated in habits of Greek thought, for their own sakes and also on behalf of those who attempted the intellectual's approach to the Christian creed, and on account of those too who derided it, people began to inquire what Plato, Aristotle, or their descendants like the Stoics had to say to the Church, and whether Philosophy and Faith could talk with one another. Justin stands at the head of a long line of thinkers who have built up and still are building up Theology. And down in Africa, Tertullian was asking himself what could be said of Christianity by a citizen of that Empire who was above all, and Latin-wise, a lawyer and a soldier; and Catholic ethics advanced rapidly under the impetus he gave.

But in that selfsame Africa, not least in the enormous polyglot, sensual yet mystic-minded city Alexandria, a conglomeration of sects was seeking fusion, and found it in terms of Gnosticism, with its contempt of matter, its panting towards vision, its inner circle of the "Know-ers", the Illuminated, compared with whom the average man was negligible religiously. And when Neo-Platonism and Neo-Pythagoreanism had mated with this, the true rival Religion stood forth, complaisant toward all forms of paganism because it deemed it could so easily transcend while using them. Before that, Irenæus had made the first synthesis of Christian doctrine, and had set it, *as* doctrine, over against the Gnostic individualistic illuminism: but the contest was not finished and the Church has ever had to fight against false rationalism, false mysticism, against electicism, and syncretism. Clement in the wake of Justin, and Cyprian in that of Tertullian, did work at which none should sneer, even though above them like Alp above hillock towers Origen with his Hebrew, Oriental, Egyptian, and Greek culture, and in him an era closes.

We see, then, in this first period emphatically not a time of fusion, or of absorption from this side or that, but a time of fierce self-preservative resistence: and if it be said that on the occasion of this or that attack, Christianity developed something it already possessed from the outset, because it was invited or forced to work upon it, this is very different from saying that it borrowed that very thing from its environment. It would be far better to use the other fashionable paradox, and say that if early Christianity is Catholic, it is so because Catholicism is pre-Christian, a notion which, were we writing on the history of religions at large, we should have, we trust, no great difficulty in clarifying. "Fiery spirit, freezing intellect, melting emotion", then, tested the young Church, and none of these altered its structure or vitiated its instinct or perverted its mind, let alone made an end of it.

When the Church emerged from her catacombs, having made clear that whatever death-wounds the Lamb suffered from the Dragon, it would never die, and that the Beast, Satan's Vicar, was and would be throughout history but the parody of Christ whom it sought to imitate in order to attack Him, the eternal struggle entered on its new phase as between Byzantium and Rome. Feverish with Asiatic infection though the Greek world now was, anæmic though the firm-skeletoned Roman West might become, each still could fight the other, the Greeks thinking of the Westerns as mere boors, the Latins of the Greeks as effeminates and liars born. In Byzantium wealth and splendour and the tyrant enthroned seemed to place in the East all the promise of the future. Rome, a dying city in a ruined land, yet never hesitated to defy not Byzantium alone, nor Antioch only, but even Alexandria when any or all of them attacked that by which she knew herself to live, Christian Doctrine that by destiny she was to preserve, proclaim, and interpret.

This we watch during the era of the great theologians and the Councils. A series of great men stood forth, of whom in the Greek-Eastern half of the world Athanasius and Cyril were far more massive, even humanwise, than any emperor: round about them were others of less sublime sweep of mystical and intellectual energy, perhaps, but wise, lovable, intelligent, and very strong, like the great

Cappadocian triad and John the Golden-mouthed. No one now says childishly that these men quarrelled about an *i*. By turning their masculine yet most subtle minds on the great mysteries of their Faith, they not only ensured for the future a certain *kind* of Christianity, but, thereby, an entire civilization: moreover, by insisting that men should think accurately and express their accurate thought in exact language, they provided the Europe-yet-to-be with a mind, and with a language: and without them, there is not the least chance of our having been able to hold out against the Arabs and Mohammed. And in all history we might fail to find an example more striking than the Councils, of how Rome imposed upon the world those dogmas which it was the business of theologians to elucidate. To elucidate! Indeed they did so: yet it is to these same men that we owe not alone the intellectual statements of what can thus be stated, but the first adequate expression of the analogical value of all our statements about God, and the nature of that supernatural world in which we are called to live, and whose transcendent truths we are bidden contemplate. Thus from end to end—from the littleness and the splendour of humanity, to the sublimity and the condescension of our God, and the recapitulation of all things into Christ—swept the thought of a period which for intellectual energy and, we hold, accomplishment, went beyond the achievement of Athens in her glory, or of pagan Alexandria when the torch was hers to hold.

No less colossal among great men (such as the senatorial Ambrose, or Jerome, whose Vulgate retaught men Latin until Dante and beyond) stood St. Augustine, to whom we owe two debts especially: one, for his *City of God*, which in reality has helped us to contemplate the maximum that can be reached by world-organization—legitimately reached and, if possible, held, provided the pageant of Empire in no way blinds us to the eternal world which after its manner it symbolizes: and, the Christian notion of Will. Owing to Pelagian naturalism, with its burly northern idea that man can do, if he tries hard enough, everything for himself, Augustine attacked the tremendous problem, congenial enough in its concrete expression at least, to the Roman instinct, of the Will. He did not work the problem through: his weaker successors dealt often by preference with his own weaknesses: but though Augustinianism has been responsible for some of the pessimisms of history, Augustine at least shifted across to the West the Church's centre of intellectual gravity single-handed, and thereafter the vocal Church was Latin.

The northerners then came down upon the Empire rather like the "Greeks" upon the Mycenæan civilization and were quelled by what they conquered. The foci of resistance in the West were ever the same: the Pope; the bishops with their cathedrals; the supreme educative force in Europe, Benedictine monasteries. Gregory and Leo; Isidore, Columbanus, Bede—but it is not a list of names between Romulus Augustulus and Charlemagne that matters: we must insist that these ages, if dark, are very starry ones, and that the angels of these stars are the churchmen. If we may hazard a guess, we should say that the more this neglected period is studied, the more surprising will be the element of civilization, due to the Roman religion, that will be found in it. Certainly immediately after Charlemagne, in the worst of the tumult, the organizing energy of the Church (Alcuin) and its general intellectual level (Raban Maurus, Paschasius Radbert of Corbie, Agobard of Lyons), and even its sudden flares of genius—erratic, if you will—like that of John Eriugena (a Neoplatonist born too late?), cannot possibly have grown up out of nothing. A secret but very vigorous and continuous past is postulated by them. And a great proof of vitality is given by that which constantly renews itself and even reforms itself without structurally altering itself. Such was the religious life and even scholarship of Italy, guided not only by a Monte Cassino but by Greek-speaking monks and by a brilliant Peter Damian who scourged paganism in a Latin he never could have learnt without it.

During the next two hundred years we can watch the Church struggling still with the chaotic material supplied to it, till for a brief space the eternal principles of Order and of Right for which she stood, as shown forth in the person, and uniquely perpetuated in the work, of Jesus Christ, seemed to be everywhere admitted. Admitted, I say. I do *not* say put everywhere and equally into practice, even among churchmen: but to admit a principle is at least the normal prerequisite to its application, and that application was wide and strong. Anyone can collect a muck-heap out of the material offered him by every century: still, you ought always to seek that by which a thing lives, not that by which it dies: and I should contend that in the Middle Ages the principles are those that make for life, whereas those that men substituted for them were not. Anyhow, through the ill-managed intellectual effervescence of the eleventh century, men reached that Century of Origins, as the thirteenth has most justly been called. Universities arose, compared to which for real intellectual vigour we wish that we had any nowadays: we refuse to admit that observation and research failed to go hand in hand with speculation and deduction in the persons of, say, an Albertus Magnus, a Peter Lombard, an Alexander of Hales: it is Roger, not Francis, Bacon who should be called "Father of Induction". And if the colossal genius of Aquinas, equal to whom we suppose no man has stood forth since, just as none surpassed him (taking the sweep of his mind universally) in bygone ages, is apt to hide from us the rest of his period's performance, we have to remember that this too was the flowering age of architecture, of poetry,

of painting, of history, of law, of science—for when else
were the great hospitals founded, and how much of their
knowledge and practice was not forgotten during the
contemptuous ages that followed, which ceased to create,
in the interests of imitating the classical age they thought
they had rediscovered? We should spend long upon that
thirteenth century, were it not that it is winning its way
back to the homage of our own.

Why did this not survive? There would seem to be a sort
of pulse in human nature, so that when for a while an idea
has dominated, its antithesis gains power : and when human
selfishness backs the new notion, it is, short of miraculous
interference, bound to triumph. No amount of papal
corruption and exhaustion of the scholastic vein of
thought could have compared with nationalism, expressing
itself almost at once in royal tyranny, as disintegrative
force. Canon Law and Civil Law became pitted one
against the other : for any one papal encroachment on the
civic area, state absolutism began once more to make its
dozen in both areas alike. And while it is a pity that the
Church should outstrip its mandate in dictating to a Cæsar,
when Cæsar sets his claws into divine things the disaster
is worse not in amount only, but in sort. On the top of
this came the rediscovery of Greece, and not even that
would have mattered had not men who sought to imitate
her art, sought also to live once more by her principles.
The cult of Nature was resumed, and worse than resumed,
for it was no mere "natural nature", so to say, but nature
de-supernaturalized. But thus to go back is impossible and
means death : and soon enough the Renaissance putrefied.

Meanwhile the various religious revolutions were taking
place. Luther applied the match of his rhetoric to various
trains of powder, and political, social, and moral explosions
occurred. His turbid genius created nothing new : his was
in reality revolt against authority as such—first against the

agents of the Pope, then against Papacy, then against the
Council to which he looked for help: against Antiquity,
against Scripture itself when it clashed with his impressionism. Despite the effort of Calvin's French logic to
freeze into shape the tumultuous streams, subjectivism
triumphed, and it was not so much this or that intellectual
position that was stormed, as the intellect itself that was dis-
lodged: not Rome that was defeated, so much as Authority
denied. Hence indubitable religious chaos, and in fact a
new sort of Christianity. The representatives of Rome,
conscious of their bad personal example that had so
obscured the claims to obedience rightly made by their
office, began an austere period of self-reformation. Indeed,
Protestantism and Rome at this time offer perfect instances
of Revolution and Reform. Again, driven back within
her trenches, the Church had to insist constantly on
Apologetics and controversy, rather than proceed happily
constructing, developing, and adorning the Faith she had
always kept and desired to preach. Hence the gradual
apparent divorce of theology from general interests, or
what came to be known as "science". None the less, at
this very time she was prolific more than ever in the fruits
of the Faith, namely, Saints—Teresa, John of the Cross,
Philip Neri, Ignatius of Loyola, or Francis Xavier. The
list might be very long. Though in some parts she main-
tained her position, consolidated, and even recaptured it,
yet even there nationalism, still expressing itself in
Cæsarism, was secretly reproducing the old principles of
the ancient duel: it is remarkable that just where such tyran-
nies reached their logical consummation, the revolution
came most violently about. Added to this was the invasion
of philosophy itself by subjectivism, which, by way of
France and then of Germany, has permeated the whole
world. When the social revolution had reached and rooted
itself after a special fashion in the ex-Protestant countries

too (for to-day there are no Protestant ones left), the modern world had fully come to birth, with its supreme problem, Authority versus Individualism. For either there is no Authority, and then you have anarchy; or, you have a God-less State-Authority, such as was aimed at in Nazi Germany and, as we write, prevails in Russia where individual life counts for nothing at all, and conscience for less than nothing: or, you have a legitimate secular authority, recognising a spiritual Authority in the spiritual sphere, which, far from injuring civic life, can but make men into better sons and better citizens.

Catholics must be forgiven for seeing in the Church alone, positive principles of construction, principles that are of an ultimate and abiding sort. There never has been the time when the Church had not to oppose absolute Cæsarism, whatever form Cæsar took at the moment: nor the time when she had not to rebuke self-sufficient rationalism, nor be on her guard against volatilizing mysticisms. She has her own system and theory of Just Government, of the powers and limits of Reason, and of the glorious perilous magnetism of Mystery. She caters for all these things, and restrains their extravagances and refuses autocracy to any one of them. Chiefly in the sphere of education is she now resisting the invasion of Conscience by the State: she still has to deny the claims of dictatorship made by such Victorian-wise optimist scientists as survive, with that talk of theirs concerning Laws of Nature for which modern students grown suddenly all-too timid are substituting everywhere "my endlessly corrigible hypothesis"; and she sees with the greatest apprehension not only the quaint new cults, backed largely by rich and idle persons on whom the Nemesis proper to materialism is taking its revenge, but, much more seriously, the vague philanthropic idealism which is debauching the intelligence and even the will. She will never forget that older Rome

which went down in the golden haze of syncretism, while
a bland Sun-god shone down upon all men alike, fusing
systems of philosophy firm-articulated even when mislead-
ing, and letting the will slacken into amiable conven-
tionality in public, while it reverted to brutality where none
could see.

The Catholic, then, holds most definitely that a new
thing came into the world with Jesus Christ: first of all,
Himself; and then, with Him, the knowledge and deliberate
appropriation of divine Grace and the supernatural life.
Ever since then this has worked in our complex world, with
as strange-seeming results as yeast can have when it
works within a paste. Since Christ willed that so His
Church should work, since it was never to be divine at the
expense of being thoroughly human, no Catholic can possibly be disconcerted at the sight of all the human miseries
that beset it. As each individual knows all too well that
Grace has not yet finished its work within his own soul, and
also, that it is he as often as not who prevents Grace working very much faster, so no Catholic supposes that the
Church has finished her work within the world, and also, he
knows that it is the sins of her own representatives, or at
least their limitations, quite as much as those of her enemies
or of the indifferent, that are responsible for much of her
slow progress. Moreover, the Church has that heavy work
of always beginning again, if only because the generations
recur, and recur already different from a decade gone.
But the pulse, the throb, the cycles of life and death that
we observe, are only to be expected by one who knows that
the life, death, and resurrection of her more-than-model,
her Indweller, Jesus Christ, are for ever to be reproduced
in her till His final triumph. The Wild Beast wars against
the Lamb: the World-Wanton flouts the Eternal Bride.
The Holy City is besieged: she withdraws into her ever
more narrow ramparts: at last her courts are taken and

given over to the heathen who trample them under foot. Only the innermost sanctuary remains—only the double work of Witness and of Sacrifice, of Teaching and of Mass. Who knows, for a brief moment even her Witness may seem to have been slain, her altar overturned. But she would arise once more, stand upon her feet, and renew herself, and without doubt God would be found to have had, even then, many a prophet hiding in the crannies of His world. Therefore the Church, human and divine, is seen by us as substantially affecting all that the world contains, without destroying it; and as herself bruised or bedecked by all the world contains, and not destroyed by it. Why the past has been just what it was, he may surmise: what the future will be, he is wise not so much as to guess. God is eternal, and His promises endure.

PART IV

THE CHURCH IN THE WORLD

I WAS accustomed in my childhood to the oracle that "there will never be another Pope". Since then, however, the spiritual authority of the Holy See has been constantly on the ascendant. Now, however, the Church has suffered so many reverses in so many countries of recent years, and ever-expanding State-monopolies seem to be encroaching so fast upon her liberty, that not a few declare that she can have no future, at anyrate in Europe. Nor would I be reluctant to expect that she will come to bear an appearance less and less European.

1

The history of the Church has been far from merely European. There exist today many oriental communities in union with the See of Rome, and their immemorial Rites are intangible according to the normal Law. I believe that some dozen such Rites are celebrated daily within Rome itself. Yet, given the fact that missionaries often could hardly but think that their own civilisation was better than what they came into (not to insist on pressure from Governments), missionaries of limited imagination carried abroad with them, besides the Faith, much that was European in appearance and even in substance. We can hardly doubt that it was as unwise, for example, to put up a perfect little French hospital in a Japanese village, as to erect sacred images in a Mohammedan land : to insist on African Natives living in square huts when they want to live in round ones (which are indeed in every way preferable) as to seek to abolish dancing or to initiate them into a music which after all oniy about a third of the world understands and is quite alien to theirs. But on the whole, it is not Catholic missionaries who have carried a foreign "culture" into other continents, but traders and government officials, who too often have brought also guns, alcohol, diseases, and new vices, and for reasons of gain have created new needs, professing thereby to introduce "civilisation". We have, in fact, heard civilization defined as the creation of new "needs", the "needs" in this case being gramophones and the radio. It is, however, pleasant to know that the Holy See which for long has urged the development of native clergies and hierarchies (at the time of writing, Java, I think, is the only place to have a Catholic bishop both of whose parents are Mohamedans), applies the same principle to the much subordinate sphere of art, encourages the drawing or carving of holy figures entirely according to native traditions, and deprecates the building of churches in Gothic or Romanesque style in, e.g., China. Artistically, what may be feared is a sterilised art—lest Natives should imitate European motifs, or, worse, lest Europeans should copy native styles unaware of the spirit that created them. Much more significant, I think, is the ever deeper study of Indian and other oriental philosophies that is now going forward: missionaries no more think that they enter lands where they have everything to give and nothing to learn. Looking eastward, then, I daresay that the Church will speak with less of a western "accent", while I should be sorry indeed the *Romanae maiestas aurea linguae*—the stately, sonorous and exact Latin tongue—failed to recapture something of its universality as an international tongue in this part of the world. All this is the more true since I should say that any directly European influence in the Missions or India, parts of China, Egypt and the Arab world—to say nothing of whatever Palestine will become—cannot but steadily dwindle.

Looking westward, no one—even though not indulging in the fatuity of prophecy—can fail to see in the United States of America a world-influence bound to increase. Probably we can afford to discard the word "isolationism" in regard of them, as they can the word "imperialism" in regard of us. They can no more maintain the one, than we can, or wish to, reproduce the other. I am not speaking of influence on subordinate (yet culturally far from unimportant) planes, such as that exercised by the cinema which is affecting, and quite possibly infecting, every continent. (One should have seen the impression made by inferior films upon Arabs or Croats. They would have been innocuous and even boring to ourselves: but in them they excited many an evil and violent passion.) But I refer to a certain *sort* of vitality, or perhaps a less hampered vitality—less hampered both in fact and in imagination—than ours is. In every civilisation, as it matures, there is the risk of getting tied up in precedents, methods of procedure, diplomatic formulas, which reduce documents almost to unintelligibility, delay action, and dishearten the energetic. When technique, common sense and vision come simultaneously into play, it is almost always the first that wins! Still, a high standard is never reached slickly: each stage must be laboriously attained to: and we hope that Europe can still supply a maturity which is not softly over-ripe, nor dustily mummified. As for Latin America, we must earnestly trust that it will not abandon its precious heredity for the sake of any shoddy imitation, or of mere mechanisation bringing the loss of what is spiritual and of beauty, the consequence of the spirit. We can hope, then, from America, for much free joyous *creation*.

In all this, I repeat, we are not "prophesying", but trying to suggest some of the material which apparently is awaiting the activity of the Catholic Church, and the kind of inter-mediate formations that we may expect, given that yeast does not turn dough instantly into bread. The mass writhes and bubbles within itself and remains for a long time quite unappetising. As for Europe, long before either war it had been intellectually in disarray within itself: there was no common mind within even one country—even Spain, where a very proud individualism is none the less conscious of a very noble tradition. Had there been no wars, I could imagine the countries having become still more conventional in their maintenance of religious forms, so that when persecution of any sort arrived, only Catholics by conviction would remain loyal to their Faith and to the Church, while others, seeing that there was no centre of stability or true source of spiritual life other than the Church, would become converted to her. Thus in tradition-ally Catholic countries, the Church would grow weaker; in non-Catholic countries, stronger. In fact, there would be no "Catholic countries", and that would be no bad thing. It would be impossible to say: "I am a Pole, or Irish, and therefore a Catholic: I am Danish, or Prussian, and therefore Lutheran". It would not only be as silly, but as sensible, to say: "Romanism is Italian, and so, unsuited to the English", as to say that Zionism does not suit the Zulu.

But, we hold, persecution has arrived, partly bland, partly brutal. St. John in his Apocalypse, describes both sorts in terms suited to his day, but also, suited to the two recurrent types of persecution to which the Church will doubtless be subjected to the end of her history, that is, of this world. There is the "sweetly reasonable" type, which asks merely that Nature be de-supernaturalised. Ethics are to be substituted for the Church's Holiness: propaganda will replace her apostolic vocation: inter-nationalism will be more practical than her naïve hopes for universality; uniformity will be a far better "note" of the perfectly constituted new world than her delusive "unity". And State-philanthropy will succeed where her "charity" has so noticeably failed. But should the Church continue to proclaim her doctrine and prove intransigeant, the Beast, for all it has "horns like a lamb", will soon enough "speak with the voice of the Dragon" and show a dragon's claws. Catholic education, to start with, is to be made so difficult as to become impossible: and the family (together with its self-expression in property) will be in every way yet further weakened in favour of the State—for after all, State-Monopoly—State-worship—is what the gentle-speaking Beast aims at as truly as the roaring and ravening Beast "from over-seas", as St. John, looking from Asia, calls the Goddess-City Rome. The fiercer form of persecutor does not even pretend to be "just"—or rather, justice is defined as that which serves the State: even if it cynically permits Christian worship, it does so in such a way that youth shall be educated or forced out of it, while colleges are closed, religious orders dissolved, churches desecrated, seminaries abolished and the clergy and prelates arrested and even executed. And we must be clear that all of this is done with the fervour of a *faith*. A Communist French leader, M.T., said politely to a priest of our acquaintance: "Your faith has done great things—your cathedrals. Perhaps ours will do greater still!" "Oh—so you admit the need of religion?" "Religion?" he cried with horror. "No, no! But a Faith, most certainly!"

We cannot tell how much devastation we are destined to see. St. John, in his vision, saw all but the innermost sanctuary of the Temple, and the whole "beloved City", given over to the pagans and trampled under foot, and the voice of the minimum remaining Witness seemingly silenced. And indeed, Catholics have beheld the ending of some "world" often enough, and have been exterminated out of regions that once were full of them. The Church is indestructible: but she has no promise of so much as surviving in any particular land or even continent. What never will happen, however fierce the persecution, is that the Church will "come to terms" with the "world", nor re-interpret her dogmas so that they mean what they did not, nor admit for one moment the self-sufficiency of man, nor the perfectibility of human nature without divine aid, nor the substitution of any knowledge of God or law of God for that imparted to us by Jesus Christ and preserved, interpreted, and promulgated infallibly by the Church whose visible head is the successor of St. Peter.

2

Yet no Christian can be pessimist. I have constantly been told: "Only the Catholic Church knows how to deal with Saints"; and, "Only the Catholic Church knows how to cope with sinners." During the war I was continually informed: "Only the Catholic Church seems to know what to do with the average man." This seemed to me to be true, and also to cover the ground rather completely.

Anyhow, I notice, in these days when reaction from materialism, or despair of the world, is driving so many into "mysticism" of some sort or another, that eyes turn almost universally to the great Catholic classics as alone likely to give safe guidance. Or to that in non-Catholic authors which is as a matter of fact in harmony with Catholic mystical tradition. Thus the only material that holds Theosophy books together is at least not in defiance of Catholic theology. I think that the difference between the spirit and success of Catholic religious houses, or the Catholic confessional, and others, is symptomatic. But in speaking of Saints, I do not want to insist on preter-natural states, like ecstasy, but upon Holiness. Real likeness to God and habitual union of the will with Him. Natural goodness is good: and sometimes there is more natural goodness in a person who is not aiming at anything else, than in one who is as yet imperfectly succeeding in his supernatural aim. And the imperfect Saint may be at cross-purposes with his surroundings and make them feel awkward. Even a Saint may not be, as a distinguished ecclesiastic once plaintively said of St. John of the Cross, "comfortable". He may not be, as the same speaker said of the Fathers of the Desert, "quite respectable". It takes, perhaps, a very experienced eye to discern the real "stuff" of holiness in unpromising instances; but when it is found, it brings you to your knees. The present writer seemed to see it in Pope Pius X, for whom he has the utmost veneration, and in whom he sees a very great Pope, a man who almost by Catholic instinct rather than academic eminence was always right in his management of the intellectual troubles of his time, and a most *supernaturalized* man. Nor is the unerring instinct of the Roman at fault herein. *Quello lì! un vero Santo!* was the unanimous and quite unexpected cry of a crowd of Roman chauffeurs when I half-casually mentioned his name. Frankly, I fear that the whole conception of what a Saint is, is escaping the world other than the Catholic: on the other hand, unsatisfactory as is the mass of Christians even anywhere, we have witnessed in our own time that absolutely astounding, universal irresistible Catholic demand for the canonization of Sister Thérèse de l'Enfant Jésus, a Carmelite nun who would be only seventy-five were she now alive, who was but a child, unknown even in her little town of Lisieux, when she entered her convent, and who remained in it for her few years of life equally and inevitably unknown, and indeed who never did or said anything whatsoever remarkable, who worked no miracles; and yet who, in still fewer years, became known from end to end of the world; was recognized, Heaven knows how, if not by hearts attuned in some strange secret part of themselves, to what she was in all of herself; so that Rome, waiving every rule, has already set her upon the altars, and found itself positively lost in embarrassment over the crowds and the gifts that poured into the city for the canonization. Were you to ask me what could be said about her, I could make no other answer save that she was holy.

If I were asked why the Church knows how to deal with the real sinner, I should say, first, that she is there *to* deal with him, because Christ is in her, and Christ came to deal with sinners. Hence her simplest minister is bound, substantially, even to say what should be said to such an one, because he takes his words from Christ, and because Christ speaks through the words. Besides this, a man who has had a Catholic education as a rule retains its directive ideas—he knows always what you are talking about— and very seldom wishes to commit suicide in the depths of his spiritual life. He has always retained some strange hope —not presumption—that he would yet be saved, and knows how, when the chance seems offered to him, to reconstitute his life of faith and his contrition. I cannot forget how, during the great influenza epidemic, I found myself with even more non-Catholics who were dying, than with Catholics. With the latter, one could go straight to the point: it made not the least difference what their lives had been: one could strip off these layers with the utmost rapidity, or rather, they fell off, and there the real stuff was to be found. The Spirit had always sung His patient hymn to ears never quite deafened to it: the Light had always shone through the clouds sent whirling by the Unholy Ghost of passion, and no mere reflected light, but a substantial flame sprang from the withered soul to meet it. But with the others—what could one appeal to? What had "God" meant? What had Christ been to them?

One could not tell. Always they had mixed up what truth
their instruction had contained, with the instructors whom
they had deserted. Usually they were willing to forget all
save the God whom somehow after all they believed in,
and to listen with reverence to the name of Christ that still
retained its halo. They would say, after a while, that they
wished to believe all that God wished them to know; that
they were sorry, if they had done wrong, because God was
good; that they hoped Christ would save them. From what?
and into what? they did not know. They could not have
assimilated the full telling: but we trust that somehow they
entered into the Body of Christ, and thus into their Lord's
joy. None the less, the experience was heart-breaking at
the moment.

But men are not mostly great sinners or great saints.
They are average—sometimes dreadfully so. They seem
incapable at first sight of even guessing the dimensions of
that vast thing that Faith is. They move, with imperceptible
oscillations, in a tiny area of ordinariness. Such a man,
left to evolve a religion for himself, will create nothing at
all: but then, the Catholic Faith is not spun out of the
fibres of any man's consciousness. If we ask for results
from a subjective religion merely, we shall be doomed to
less and less satisfaction to-day, and as things are moving.
You *must* have teaching: you must have law: and you must
have grace.

The average decent Catholic knows that all these things
are accessible to him. Manifestly he is left in no doubt
about the second—discipline is upon him always, whether
or no he submits to it. Why, the very rule of Friday abstin-
ence, not to mention that of Sunday Mass and of his
Easter duties, does much to keep him in shape. It is
perfectly idle to suggest that discipline is out of place in
religious matters. There cannot possibly be any real
reason for saying so, save that we don't want it and require

an excuse for rejecting it. What possible *a priori* reason can there be for denying the utility in spiritual matters of what all sensible men esteem so highly in all other matters? Even art goes to pieces when it has not been disciplined, whatever æsthetes say. Spiritual matters and the rest of life are not so hopelessly divorced. Indeed, I hold that nowhere so much as in these elusive affairs—life, morals, ideals— does a man need discipline. Nowhere else is every illusion of selfishness, and indeed of unselfishness, so likely and so dangerous. And civil servants have again and again complimented us on "your wonderful discipline". Indeed, they have assigned it as sufficient cause of the "success" of the Roman Church. But, they always regarded it as man-made merely: they never sought for its principles. A very famous barrister once complimented me on the other aspect of Rome—her "common sense", broad-mindedness, flexibility—basing himself on marriage nullity and similar cases he had known. I said: "You have, of course, noticed that there is an absolutely rigid skeleton of principle in all that? There has been no complaisance. You will never buy justice, let alone injustice, from Rome." He reflected, acknowledged it had never struck him, and agreed. It is just because Rome is rigid in principle, that she can afford to be adaptable: her adaptability is never that of an invertebrate.

Hence, however much the ordinary man may chafe under discipline, he knows on the whole that it is good for him, and above all he knows that it is based upon taught truth. He may say: "I'm shockingly ignorant of my religion, but I presume there's a reason for this order, and I'd like to know what it is." Then you tell him. The same holds on the whole in dogmatic things. I shall never forget a man writing to me that some dilettante had told him that Christianity was derived from Mithraism. "I told him he was a damned liar", he wrote. "What shall I say next?"

You may cry: "What priestly tyranny does not this imply! What failure to think for himself!" Not in the least. He knew perfectly well that Comparative Religion was not his business. He knew that he could not be expected, any more than his critic could, to be an expert in every department. As a waiter in a hotel wrote to me not long ago: "I only expect to have got three or four thought-out conclusions before I die: it takes you half a lifetime to see the point even of the objections." But Catholics hold that their priest, who, they knew, had been through quite seven years of careful training, would at least be able to give them the principles of the thing, even if you should not expect him, either, to be the universal expert. If at times priests seem rather careless about criticism, or unsympathetic towards critics, I think it is largely because their training enables them to see rather quickly the bearing of an argument, without knowing all the facts that concern the matter in hand: they see enough to know that even if the facts alleged be true, the objection as such is simply off the point, as when a man talks about Galileo, or the Inquisition, or Einstein, or monastic scandals. The ordinary Catholic, then, always has at the back of his head the excellent catechism he has been taught: a scheme of life, religious life, is within him, that he finds inclusive and satisfactory: if he is at all alert-minded, and thinks as well as remembers, he easily sees that other schemes cannot compare with it, and if he finds difficulties on and off, in what topic that is worth thinking about are not difficulties to be found? If such a man finds his religion "fade out", he probably does so because he has not thought about it enough, and so has not valued it, nor prayed, nor succeeded in defeating the general scenery and uproar of life.

There is, then, in such a man's life (and I am talking of quite the most commonplace man, not the reading nor the devout man) an undercurrent of consciousness that is concerned with God. He judges all his acts, however half-heartedly, from God's point of view. He says frankly: "That was a sin", not, that was a mistake, or beneath myself. He may add: "I can't see that it did much harm"; but he will not stop short there. Moreover, he does a number of things that have no sense if God be excluded as motive and sanction, as when he goes to confession; above all, when he receives Communion. His whole attitude to his clergy is explained by this: he reverences the clergy because of their office, and chaffs them or even criticizes them for their personal short-comings, just as they on their side feel not the slightest necessity for adopting an artificial voice or manner, just because they are so sure of themselves. An unpriestly priest would disgust the average layman quite as much as a clericalized layman might annoy a priest. And, possibly in consequence, both layman and priest feel very little shock, if any, in passing from a secular to a religious topic or occupation quite abruptly, so as to seem irreverent to the non-Catholic. Why should they hesitate? Either the secular topic or act was wrong, and then they were, quite simply, sinning. Or, it was right: and not only there was no chasm to be crossed to God, but God was present all along. Somewhat in the same way they can make (within limits to which they are very sensitive) jokes about religious matters. They know that the joke is, so to say, against themselves and their inadequate appropriation of the religious truth, or the hopeless disproportion between the notion or ideal and their representation of it. There is none of that frightful solemnity of philosophers who do not believe a bit in their philosophy, or of those reformers or philanthropists who know they have invented their pro-gramme or system and have to keep up its dignity and their own.

Besides this there is probably in the average Catholic so me curious streak of devotion that, if he be an Englishman (we really have not time to talk of all the national temperaments, save to say that most of what shocks the Englishman "abroad" is a more perfectly exact expression of temperament than any he allows himself even at home), he keeps sedulously to himself. Above all, the inexpressibly sacred figure of Mary keeps pace with him, and he will be slow to omit the Hail Mary even on sinful nights. I said, "above all", alluding precisely to this area of "devotion". Devotion is not Faith as such, and he knows it: what he seeks "above all" in moments of great crisis—Forgiveness, Absolution, Communion—all *that* comes from God, all that involves Christ. Take the poorest peasant of a Sicilian hillside—and I know not why these very pleasant gentlemen are constantly adduced as monuments of religious degradation—and you should catch the difference of intonation between his allusion to "Il Signore" and his appeal to "la Madonna". . . . But I can describe no longer the reaction of the ordinary man, the working, joking, sinning, straining, hoping man, to the great Catholic Thing, nor depict with any likelihood of explaining myself the constant life within him of Faith and Hope, and the incessant resurrection of his Charity.

.   .   .   .   .   .

We have, then, tried to write some pages on the Eternal and the Infinite, standing, as we do, among the shadows of this tiny transient earth; and of the Lord whom, having not seen, we love, and whom, while professing to serve Him, we but parody. We were told to display our personal feelings concerning all this. On the one hand, who, in face of such Facts, would dare to obtrude his self? On the other, in trying to write with extreme sincerity, we have no doubt quite sufficiently obeyed our orders. For we shall have shown, here and there, annoyance, and again amusement, and, we hope, our sense of helplessness, and our great content. Where we have philosophized a little, we may have seemed naïf: so be it. Our own philosophy is very simple, as we believe true philosophy must be. We could not have left it out, for it is included in the Catholic mind, and so, in a small way, in our own. We have here and there offered arguments, without developing even one of them, for we do not admit that there is a single Catholic position that cannot so be supported. On the other hand, we know quite well that arguments do not produce Faith, which is God's gift. And once and again we have half irritably, yet in fact serenely, criticized the arguments of critics, just because we, in our imperfection, felt like doing so, and, just a little, lest it might be thought we did not know of them, nor of the thousand others that are produced. But after all this, we prefer to state, praying that the content of our meaning may become ever deeper, since it cannot possibly be wider, that we believe all that the Catholic Church, the Church, that is, in union with the See of Peter, believes and teaches, and in the sense in which she believes and teaches it, because God, through Christ who founded her, revealed it, and cannot deceive or be Himself deceived. And should at any time our personal present understanding of that Faith be proved mistaken, we pray God that we may ever be ready in obedience to the Holy Roman Church, to subordinate our ideas to that Light wherein alone we see, and ever shall see, light.

INDEX

131